IMMER CALLISTO

BETWEEN 2 WORLDS

Between 2 Worlds
by Immer Callisto

For permission requests, write to the publisher at the address below.

Immer Callisto
Email: inkbyimmer@gmail.com
Website: inkbyimmer.com

Cover and Interior Art:
© [2024] inkbyimmer.com

Printed in [United States]

www.inkbyimmer.com

Between 2
Worlds

A True Tale Told in Poems

By Immer Callisto

Beware the man whose ego stands tall,
For in its shadow, pride precedes a fall.
His dependence, a treacherous art,
Can blind the mind and harden the heart.

Dear Readers,

The pages you'll journeyed through are not just a collection of poems; they are fragments of a life lived in vivid color and stark contrast. Each verse, each line, holds a piece of my truth, my reality.

From the embrace of a loyal puppy that brought light into my world, to the mystical bond with a black kitten that guided me on a path less trodden, each poem is a chapter of my life. They tell stories of love and heartbreak, of being an outcast in my own family, and of finding solace in beliefs that diverge from their own. It speak of the challenges of being misunderstood, labeled as 'crazy' for finding peace in meditation and a connection with crystals. Yet, through these verses, I also celebrate the beauty and strength found in embracing one's true self.

This is not just a book of poems; it's a window into my soul, a narrative of a journey that is uniquely mine. Each word is a heartbeat, each stanza a breath of life. As you read, know that you are walking alongside me, through the highs and lows, the laughter and the tears, the solitude and the companionship. Thank you for being a part of this journey, for witnessing my story unfold in the rhythm of poetry. In these lines, you'll find pieces of me, and perhaps, pieces of your own story.

With heartfelt sincerity,

Immer Callisto

"Seeking a love that transcends the earth,

She searches for a bond of spiritual worth.

Where hearts intertwine with celestial light,

In this journey, her soul takes flight."

IMMER CALLISTO

THE DREAMER

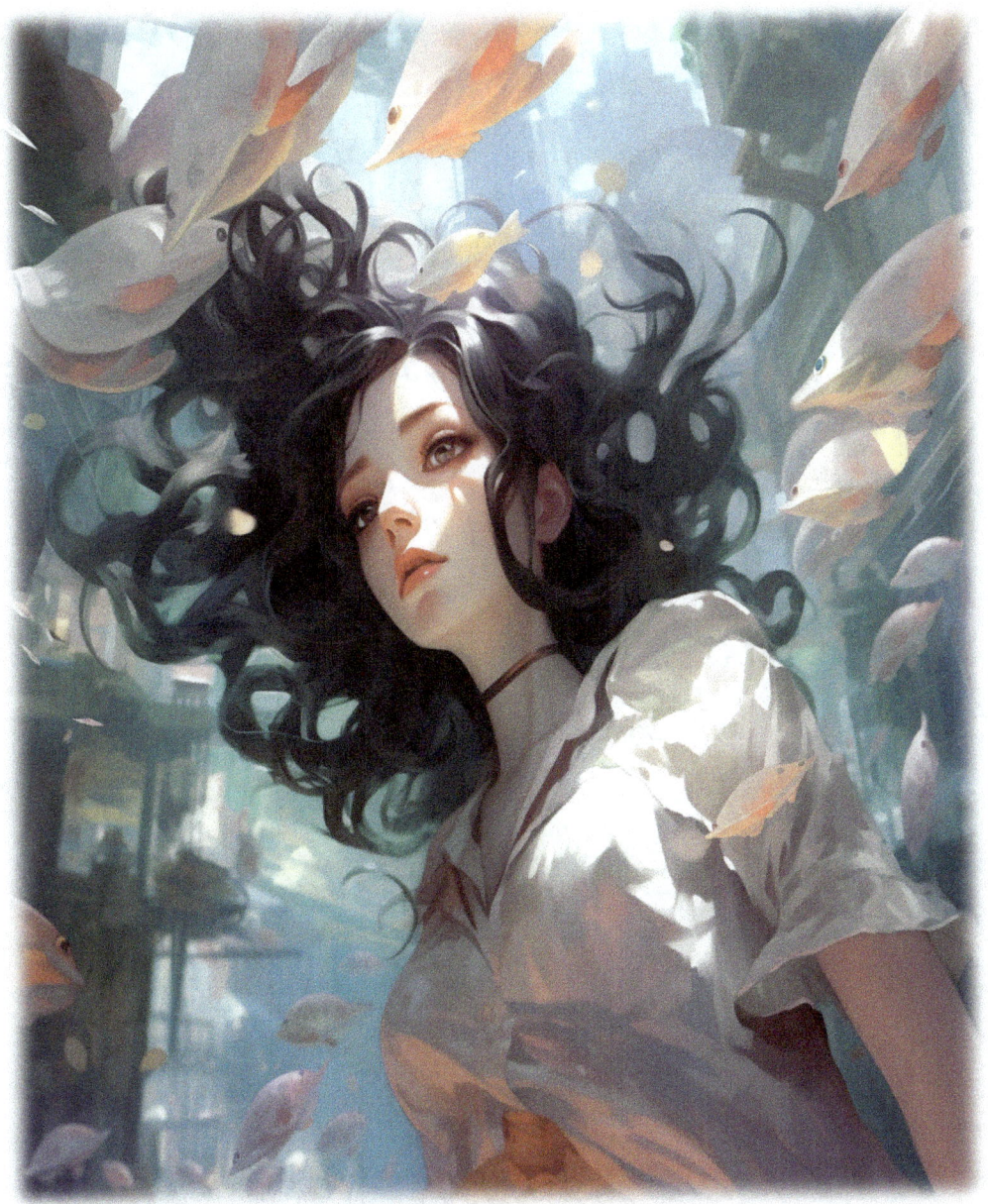

In a world awash with hues and light,
The painter dwells, crafting sight.
With every stroke, a dream takes flight,
In canvas realms of day and night.

In their hands, colors converse,
Telling tales, universe to universe.
A silent poet with a brush for a pen,
Capturing moments again and again.

IMMER CALLISTO

THE PAINTER

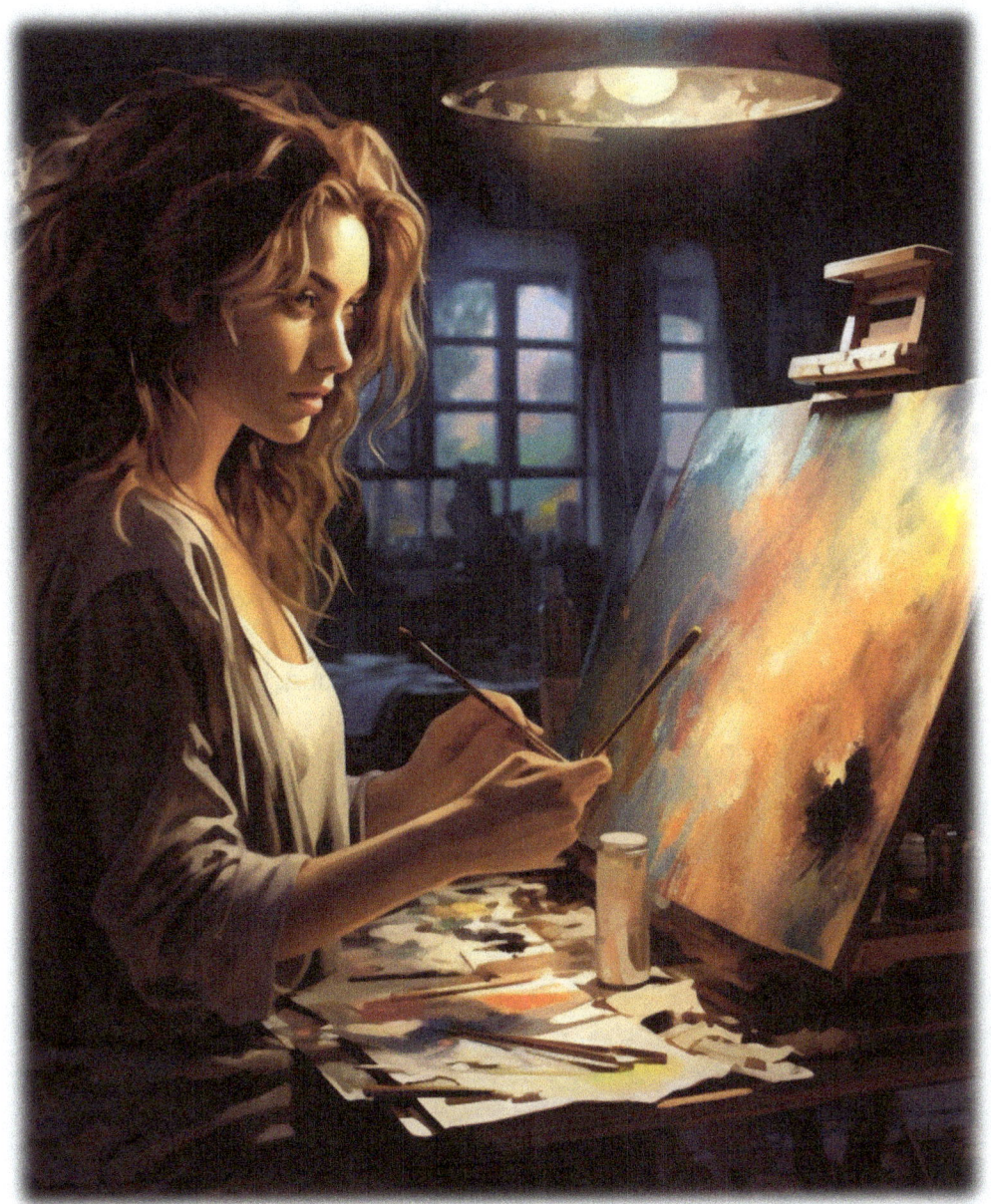

"This 1 Am"

I am forever, an endless flow,
My name, my being, this I know.
Gemini still, with countless lives,
Growling like a cat, many facades thrive.

A mystery I am, fights for the right,
Others' lives matter, in my sight.
Dreams, my truest escape they give,
Yet realism lurks where they live.

Real, but a feeling of fake it holds,
Like a matrix, its grip enfolds.
Escape seemed a dream's tale,
Yet here I am, writing, I prevail.

A book unfolds, my life's own song,
In both realms, where I belong.
Dream and matrix, intertwined whole,
Endless rope, my story's scroll.

THE CREATOR

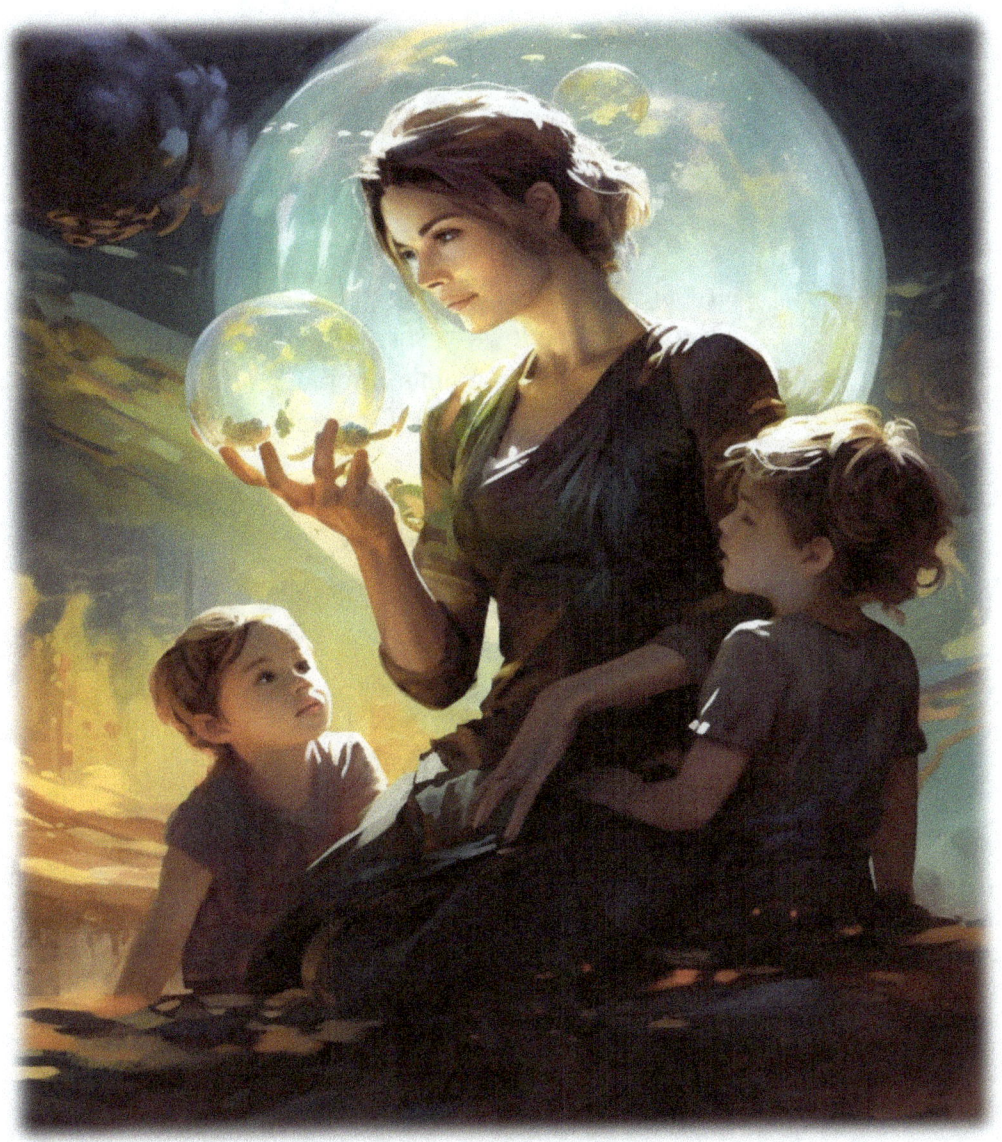

"A Fallen Beauty"

Her beauty, more than legacy's guise,
Deepens in shadows as she defies.
Each step, a spell in night's embrace,
A fragment of sorrow, not just grace.

More than a vessel, more than seen,
Her worth beyond what has been.
Marching for more than eyes can tell,
In golden chains, her silent yell.

In every step, a story's cost,
A month's labor, in gold embossed.
Crystals glisten, but can't reveal,
The heartache that she cannot heal.

IMMER CALLISTO

THE GODDESS

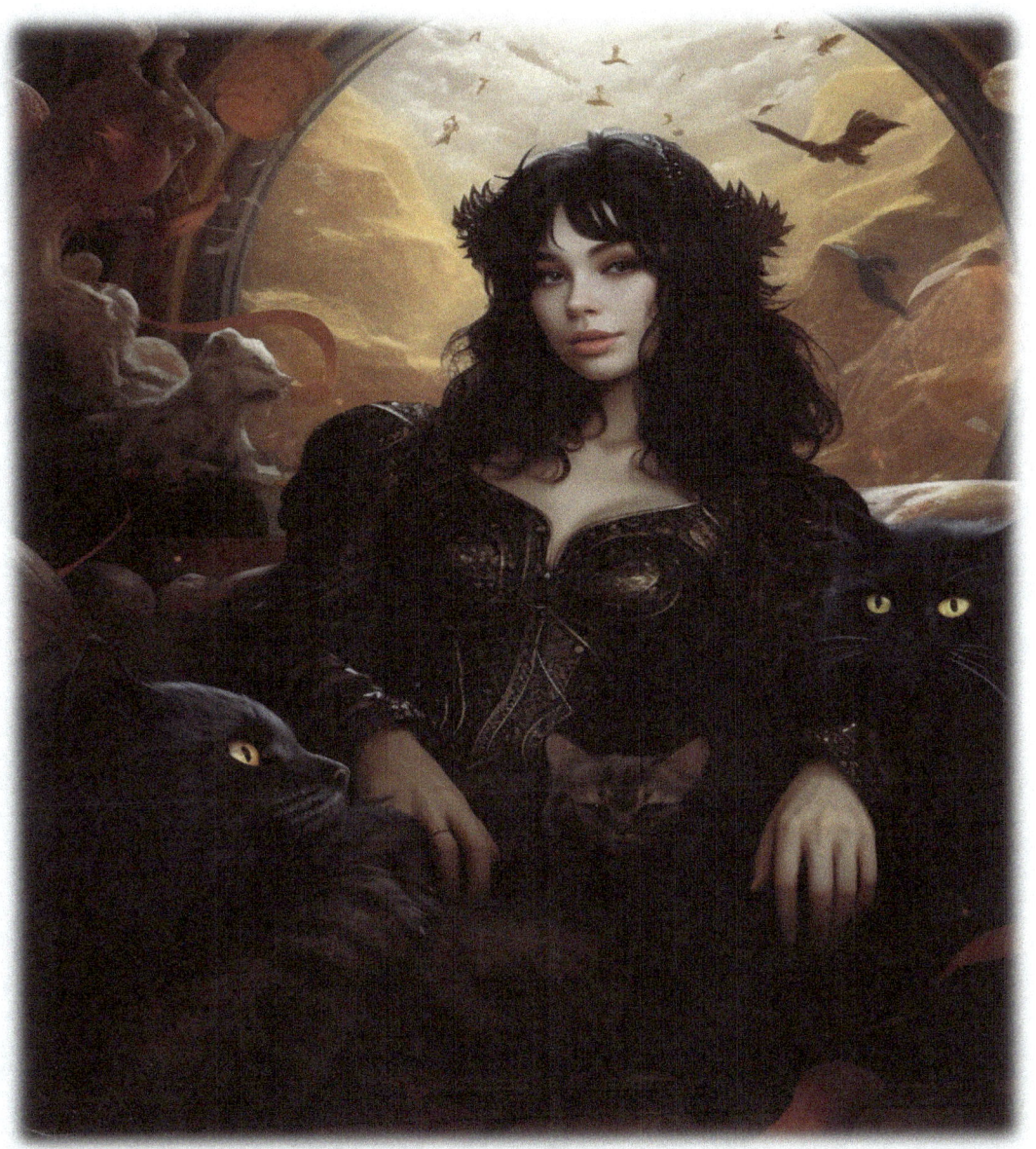

In solitude's silent embrace,

Echoes fill the empty space.

Walls whisper tales of yore,

As shadows dance on the lone floor.

THE FLOWER

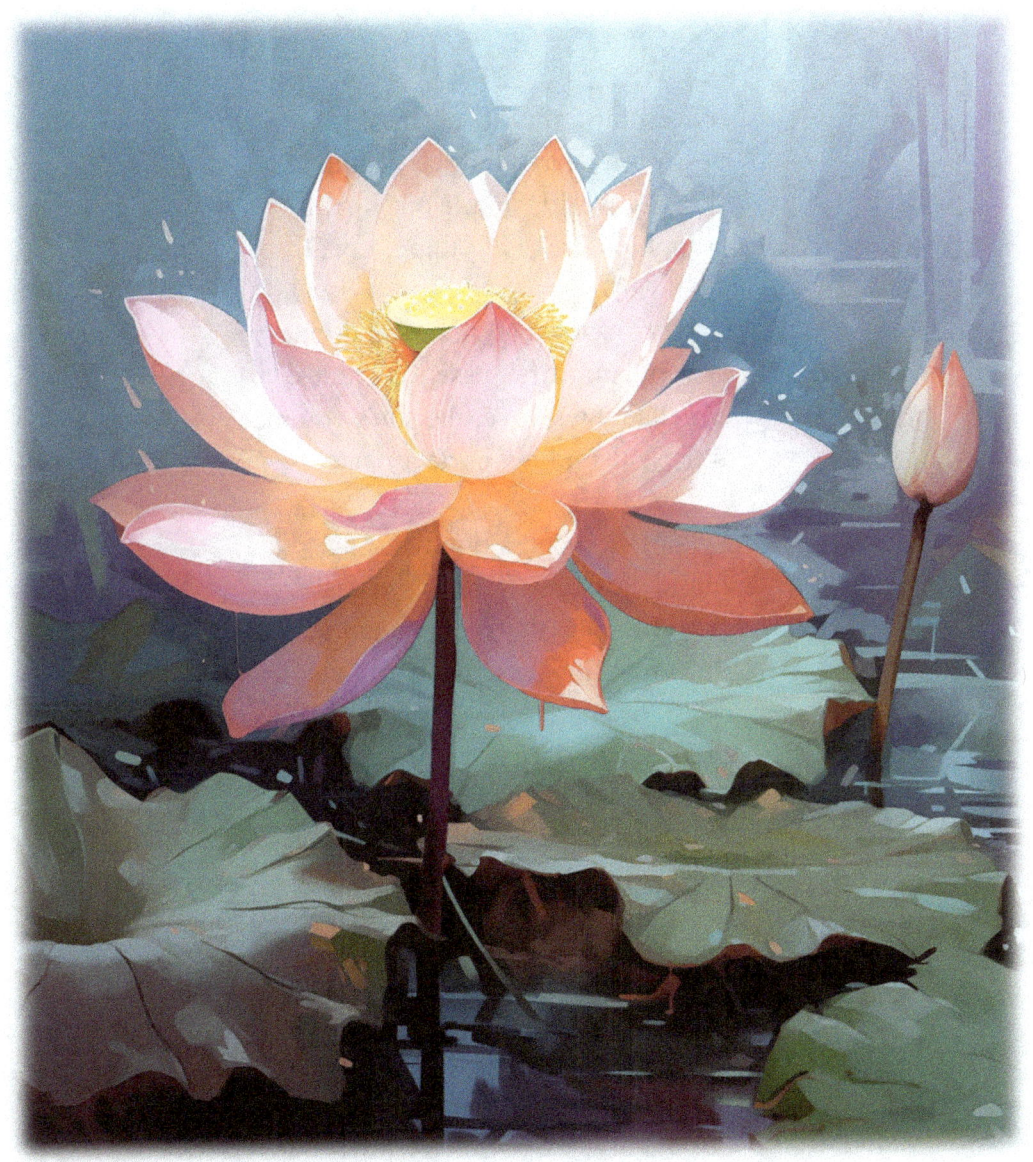

"Pursuits that Fail"

Gleaming cars, riches untold,
Desires in hearts, bold and cold.
Yet in my world, simple and small,
I find my joy, my everything, my all.

Others may chase what glitters and fades,
In their pursuit, life's essence evades.
But give me laughter, love, the sun's embrace,
In these, I find my perfect place.

A quiet moment, a book, a song,
Simple pleasures, where I belong.
Thankful for each day, come what may,
In life's small joys, my heart will stay.

Riches not in gold, but in moments dear,
In my humble world, contentment's near.
With gratitude, life's tapestry weaves,
In simple abundance, my spirit believes.

IMMER CALLISTO

THE JOURNEY

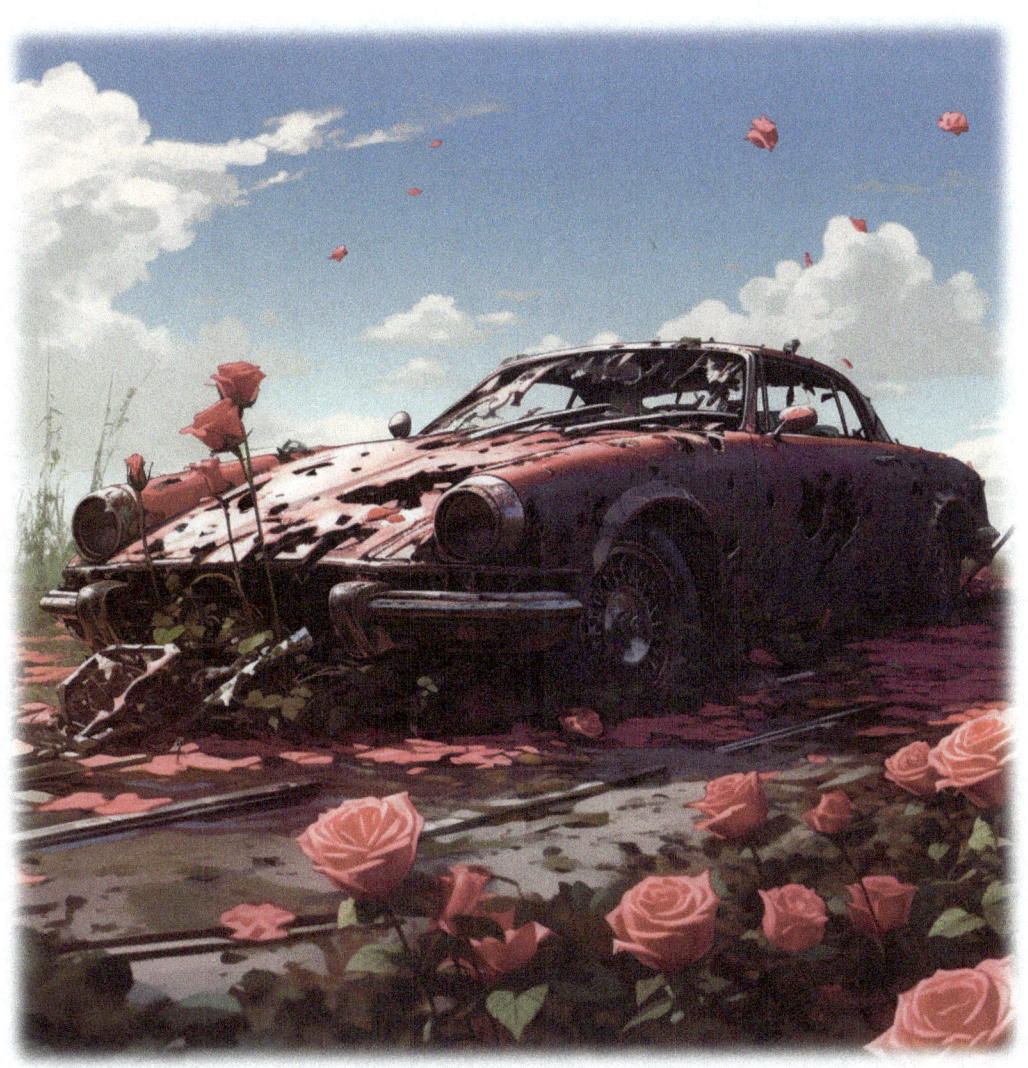

"Veiled in trust, a cheater strays,

Breaking hearts in a deceptive maze.

In their wake, trust withers and dies,

A single act, where love's truth lies."

IMMER CALLISTO

THE ECHOES

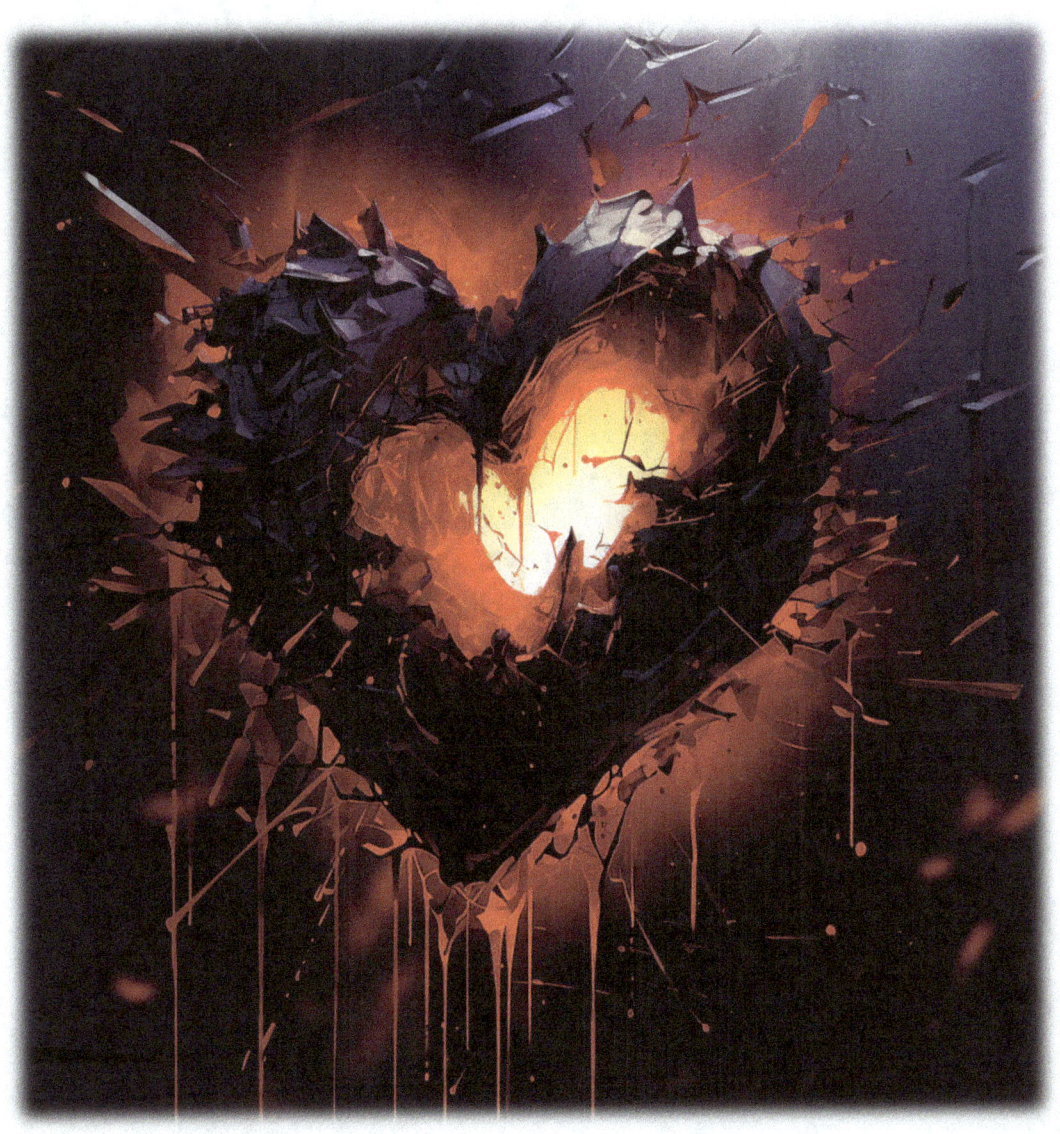

"Fading Echoes of Love"

I gave my all, heart, and soul's embrace,
He scorned it, left a gaping space.
A child he was, my love I bore,
In my hands, held, yet through me tore.

My first, perhaps sole, love's decree,
Time drifts by, my heart can't set free.
Love, it seems, forgot my name,
Lost to this bond, once aflame.

He moved ahead, I dream our goals,
Yet my path led, with little souls.
Not a mistake, my choices bless,
But this love, a lasting mess.

My love departed, a cancer starts,
Consumes my heart, rips me apart.
I'll recall the man, who broke and fled,
Never again, will my eyes be fed.

IMMER CALLISTO

THE MIRAGE

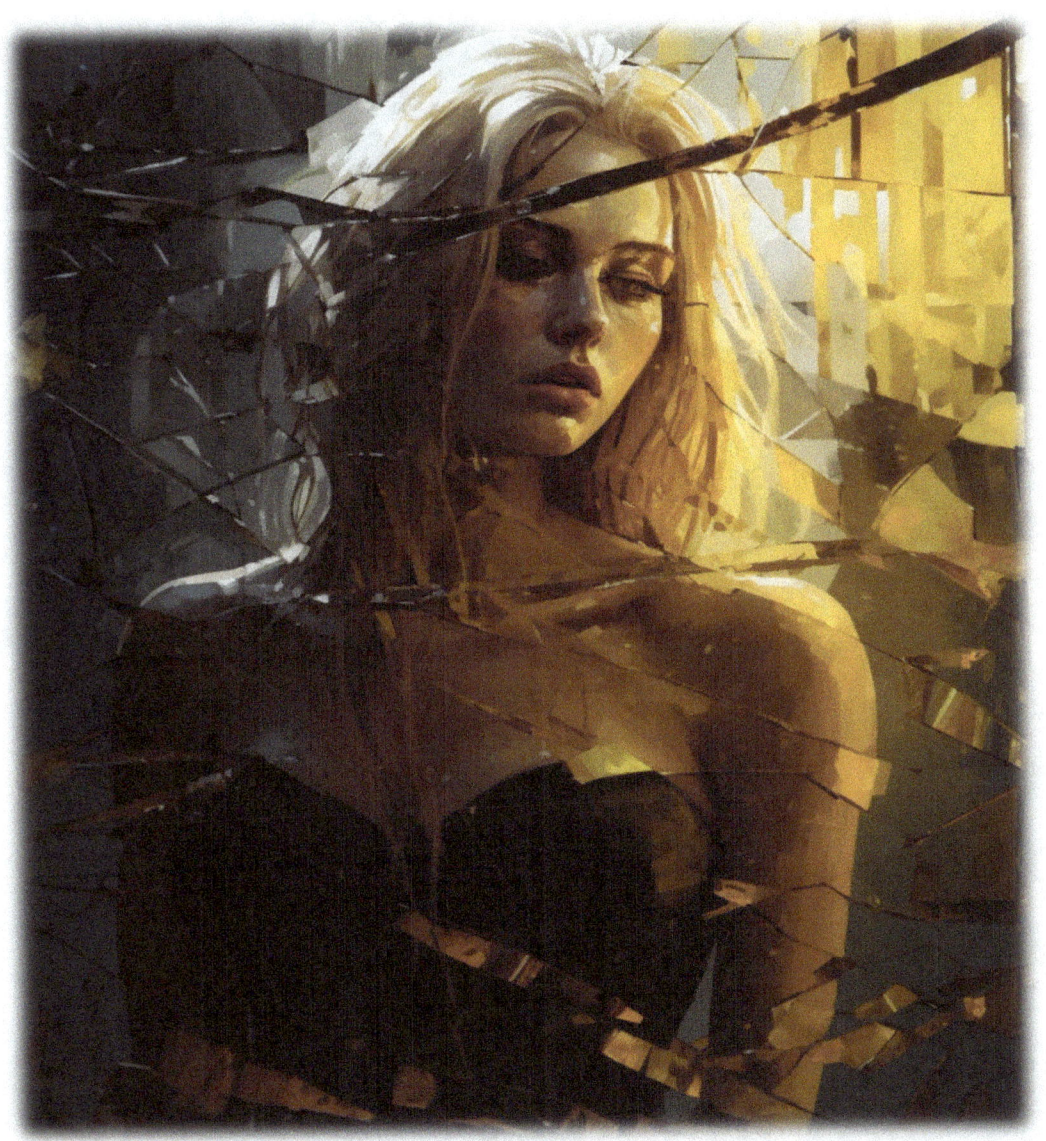

"Three Gifted Treasures"

A father of three, his knee I'd seek,
Love fleeting, abuse's havoc, so bleak.
Escaping pain, playing in fire's embrace,
His anger, a weight, my dire disgrace.

Insignificance, pain, love felt unreal,
Deserving naught, his rage's ordeal.
Yet within three, my solace found,
Peace, a love, nowhere else bound.

They, my soul's piece, we, a whole,
Connected, intertwined, heart's role.
He, part of growth, yet not my true love,
But a reminder, from below or above.

He gifted not one, but three from above,
Angels, my treasures, pure love's dove.
For him, my gratitude will always flow,
His abuse made strong, made me grow.

I walked away, raised my angels true,
His lesson learned, a life anew.

IMMER CALLISTO

THE MOTHER

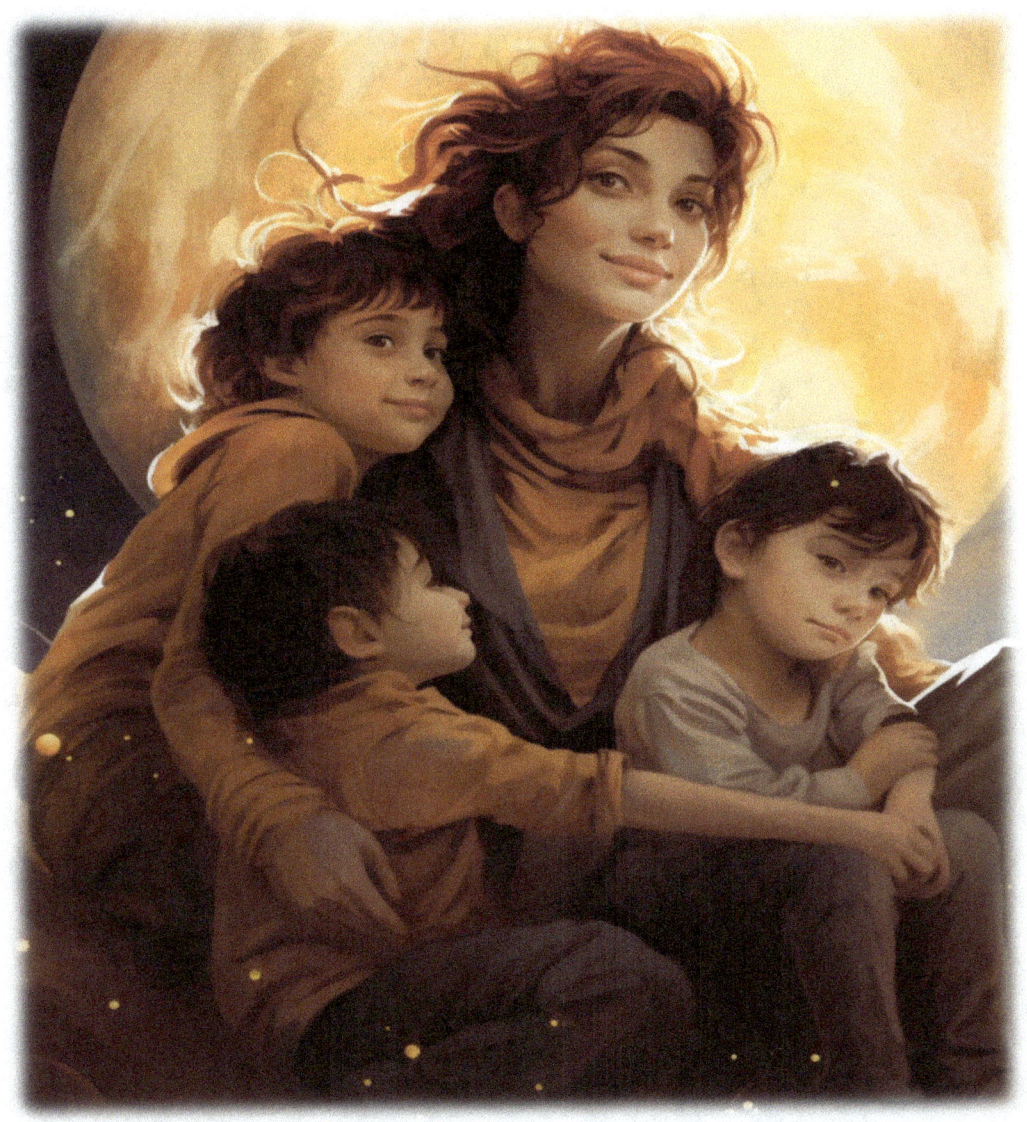

"Forever Home"

Born by the sea, on an island free and wide,
New York's embrace, a life of sorrow, pain to bide.
Cold nights, snow's bite, a piercing chill,
But fate led me where the sun's warmth spills.

To Miami's realm, sweet and untamed,
A haven found, where my heart reclaimed.
Here, reborn in the sun's tender kiss,
This vibrant place, my eternal bliss.

In Miami's embrace, my roots entwine,
A place to live, to love, to define.
From island shores to the city's beat,
This sunny haven, my life's retreat.

Here, amid the warmth and wild embrace,
I found my home, my destined place.
Born anew, in this sun-kissed dome,
Miami, my heart, my final home.

THE CITY

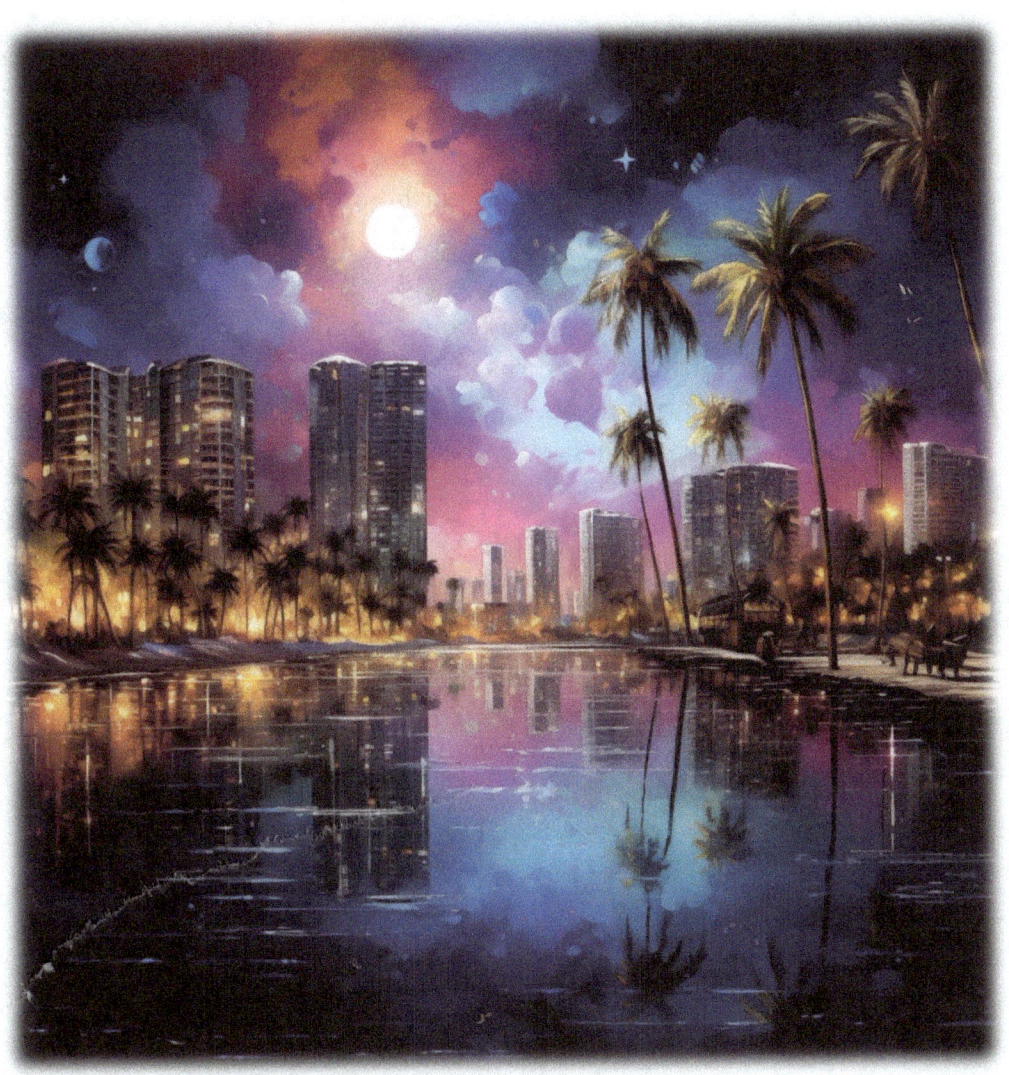

"It matters"

Respect for life in every form,
A pledge to keep, to heal, not harm.
Each creature, a marvel, earth's own art,
Deserving kindness, from the start.

Our plates, a canvas, colors bright,
With fruits and greens, a healthy sight.
Nourishing body and soul alike,
In each meal, life's respect we strike.

Gentle are the hands that tend,
To creatures and crops, a loving blend.
In harmony with nature's choir,
Our choices kindle a compassionate fire.

Healthy eating, a mindful choice,
In this act, the earth's voice.
Respecting all, both big and small,
In this balance, we honor all.

With gentle hands and hearts so grand,

Let's care for creatures of the land.

In kindness' glow, let us stand tall,

For compassion should extend to all.

Cherish the earth, her forests and seas,

In her care, we find our peace.

A respect deep, in every heart's berth,

For in her health, lies our own earth's worth.

IMMER CALLISTO

TREE OF LIFE

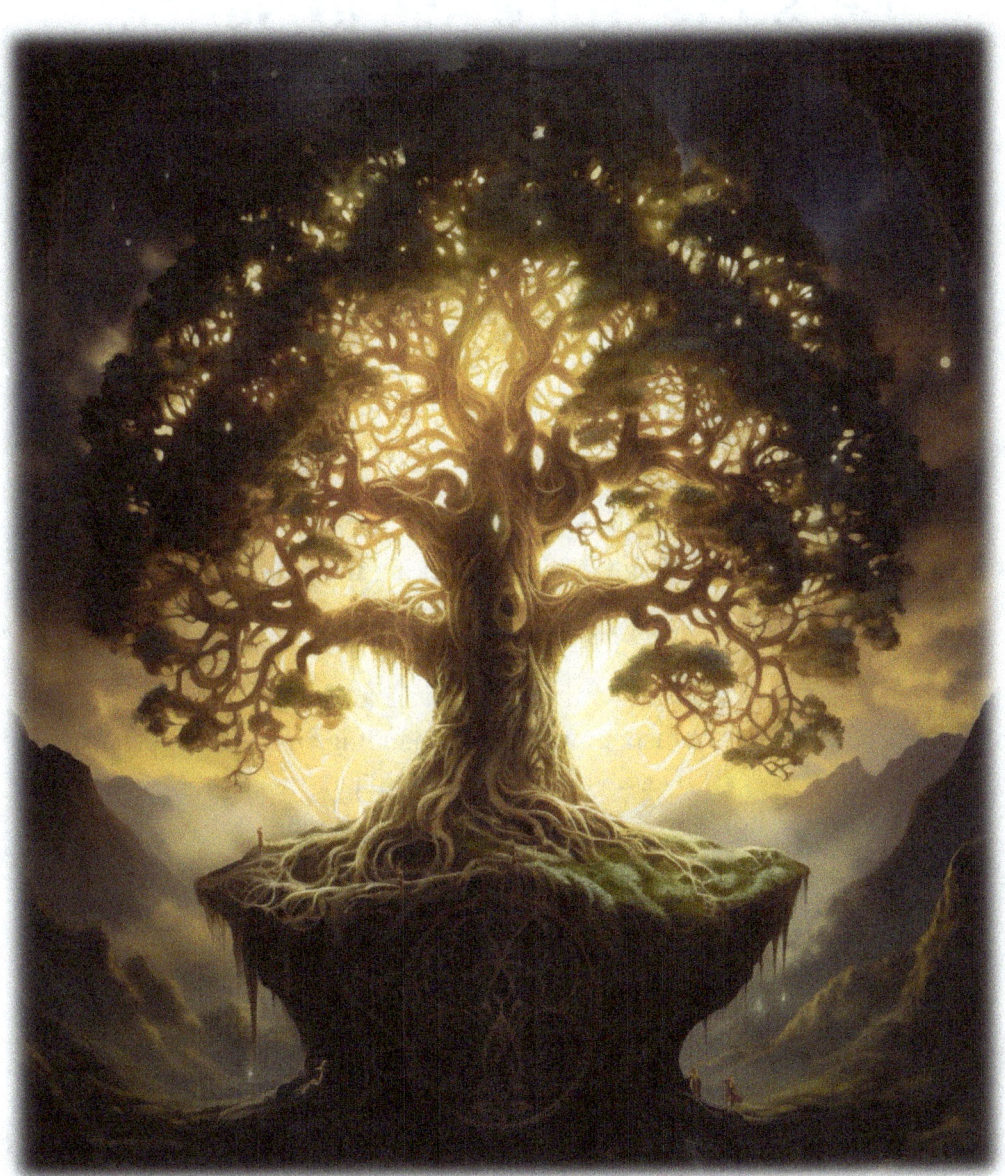

Lessons in Love's absence

She was meant to nurture, my sky above,
My haven, shelter, a beacon of love.
Light and hope, I sought in her embrace,
But found none, no compassion, no grace.

My sensitivity, her cruelty did maim,
Goals uncared for, in her heart's claim.
Belittling the weak, mocking the ill,
Her taunts, a cruel, relentless drill.

Each day, a reminder, she held the might,
In her grasp, power, a commanding sight.
Love, a void, empty and bland,
For her, wealth, the sought-after strand.

Not anger, but strength, her legacy true,
Her lack of love, a lesson to construe.
Learning to love from a loveless place,
To nurture, care, with an open grace.

IMMER CALLISTO

THE GREED

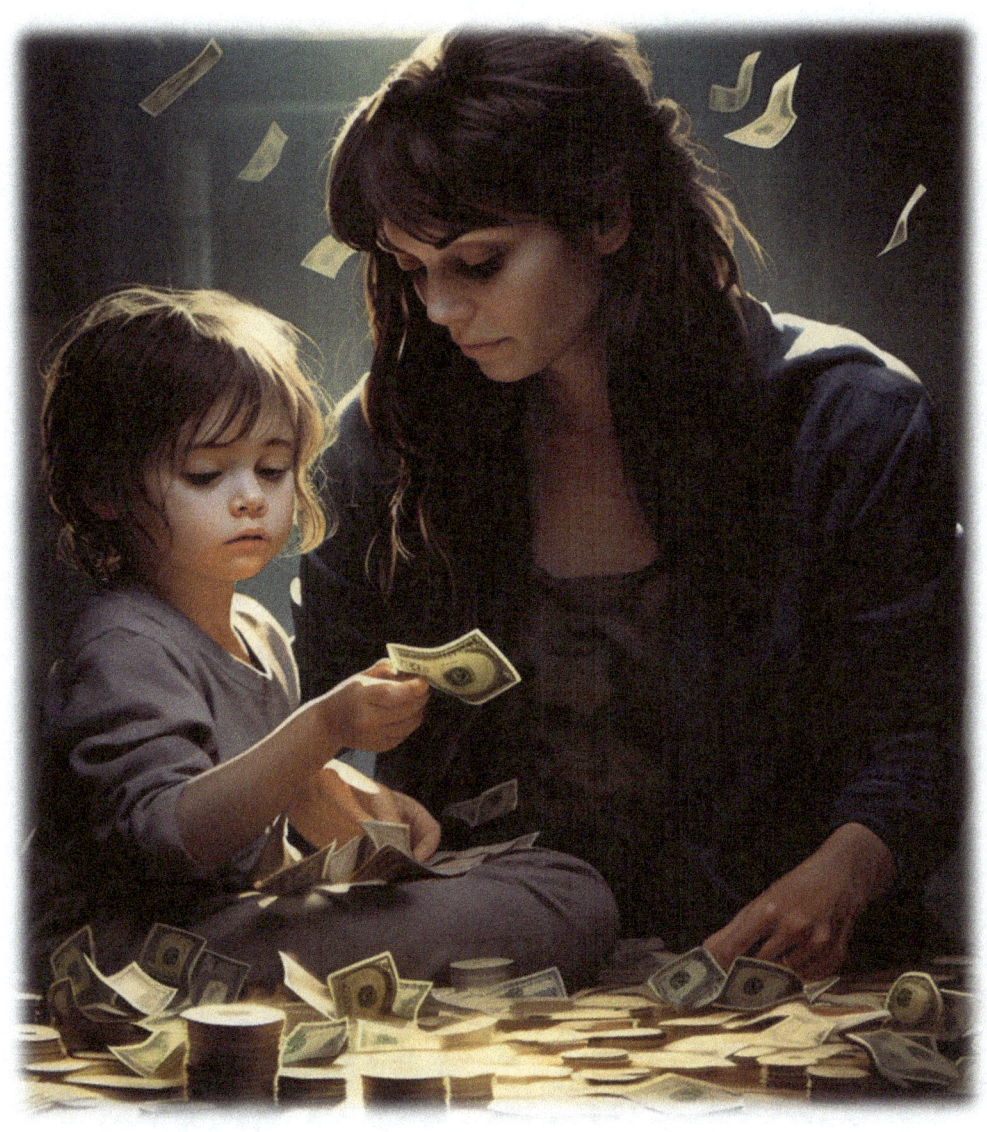

"Frozen"

Time marches forth,
a phantom's stride,
In hearts once warm,
Life relentless chase,
a shadow's play,
Our essence fades,
like dusk to-day.

Memories held,
NOW de-cay.
Overshadowed slave,
a crime escapes.
Long days long grace,
in shadows SPACE.

Survival's cruel jest,
a heart's despair,
Once bright joys,
now LOST in air.
Turned now to dust,
a silent scream,
Vanished like mist,
Of frozen dreams

THE LONER

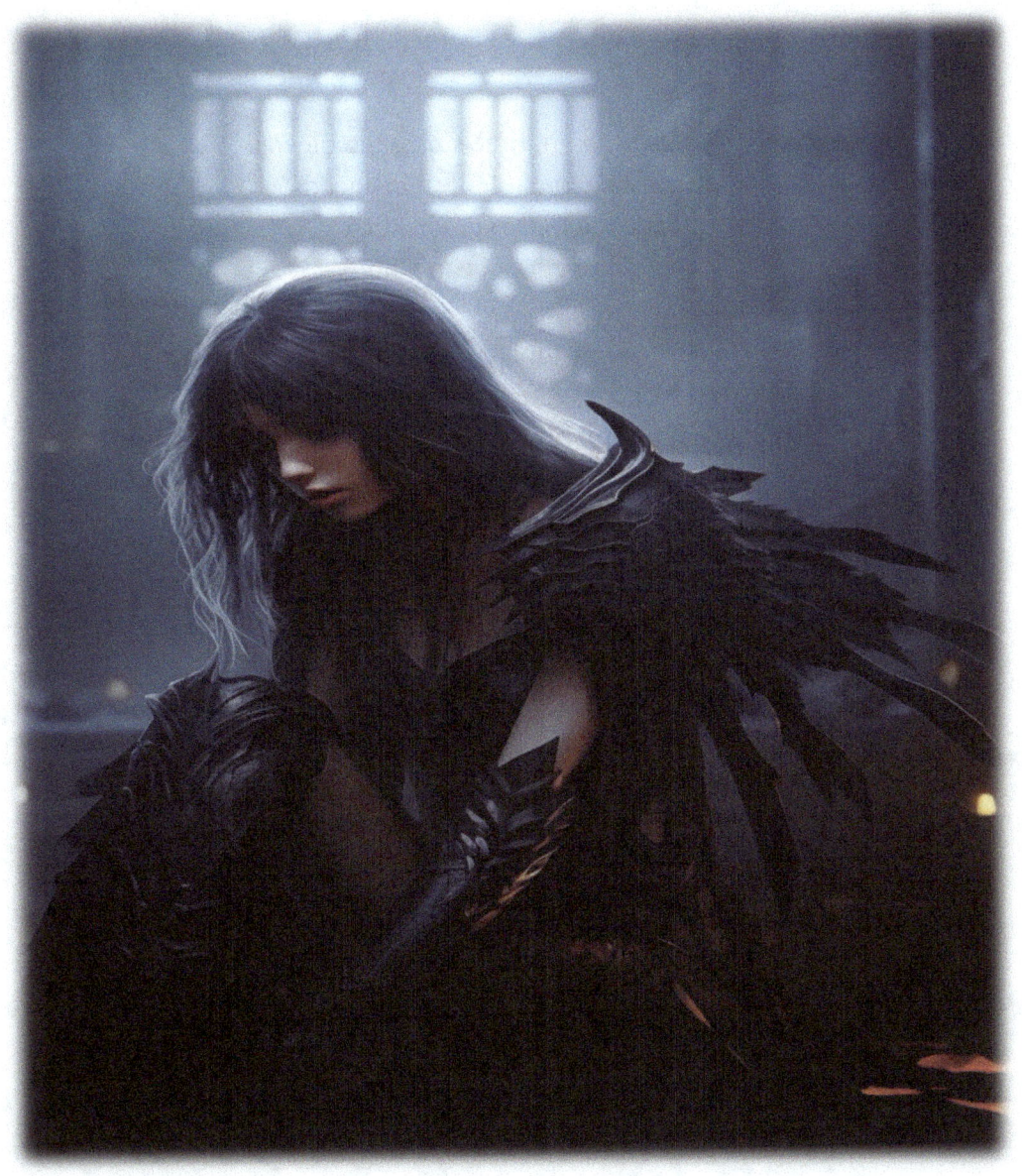

"Unrequited Love"

He, my biggest pain, time's passage bleeds,
Ripped my heart, stole it in his needs.
In his hands, my soul he took,
Turned away, my heart's nook.

Back to his birthplace, he returned,
A city of wonder, where dreams adjourned.
I chased him there, seeking love's grace,
Yet his eyes never met my embrace.

Each turn, a new lover he'd find,
A friend, he'd say, but it wasn't blind.
An empath's heart, hard to deceive,
Knew he sought others, I couldn't believe.

Soon, another replaced my place,
Gave her what with me had no trace.
Thus, I knew, my true love's lie,
A one-sided love, a painful goodbye.

I poured it all, forgotten in the race,
Left like a drop in the ocean's embrace.
Our love, a ghost, lingering, unsaid,
My bleeding heart, where it all bled.

IMMER CALLISTO

THE SELFISH

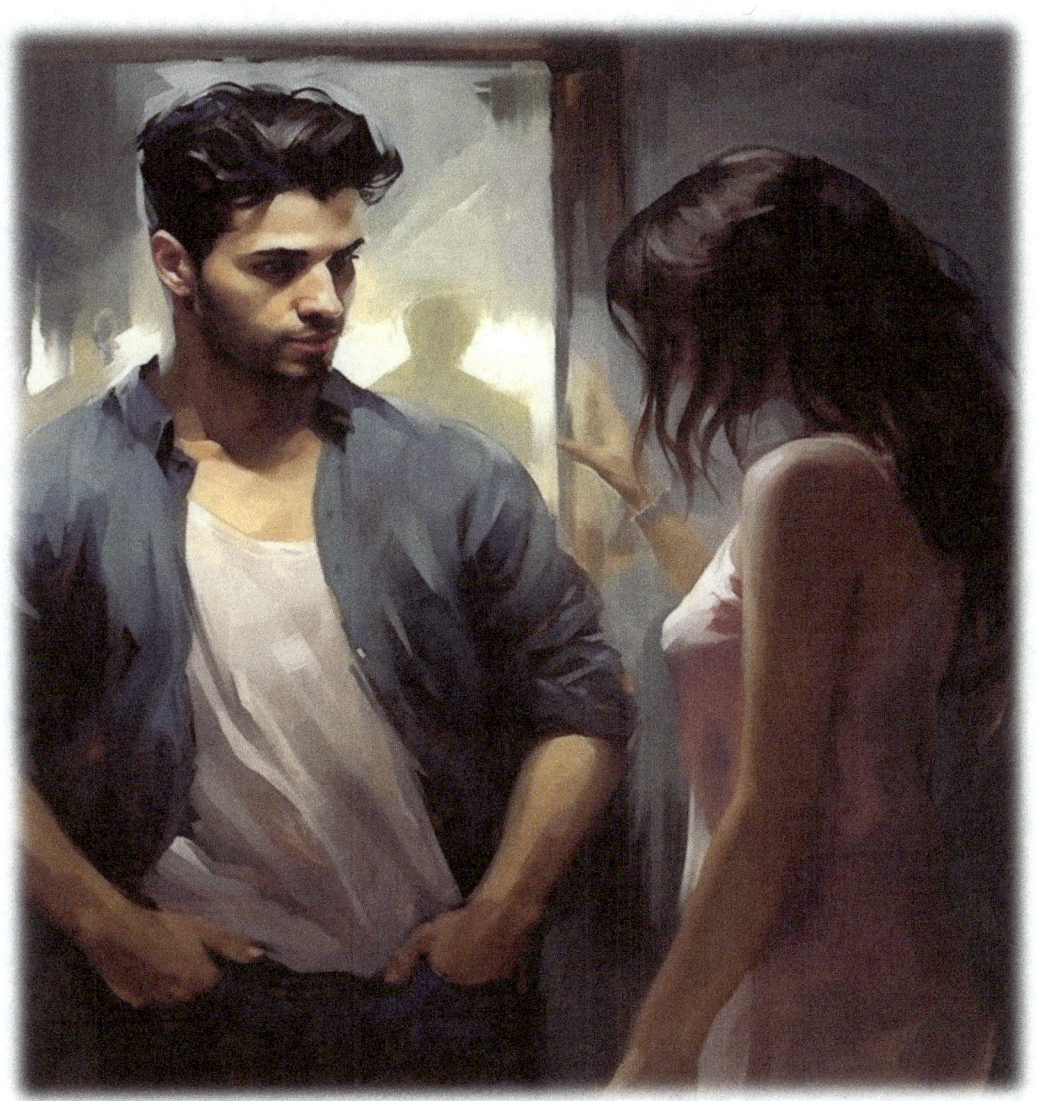

"The Ocean"

The mist clouds take form,
Sunbeams sketch the sea's calm.
But heed this well, at night transforms,
Guided by winds, its power swarms.

Away from shores where laughter rings,
In ocean's heart, a warning sign.
Treat her kindly, with gentle hands,
Or face the wrath, that she'll wave.

Anger stirs, in her vast domain,
Unleashed her fury's. It is hard to contain.
Respect her might, her timeless birth,
Or feel her rage, the earth is hers.

IMMER CALLISTO

THE OCEAN

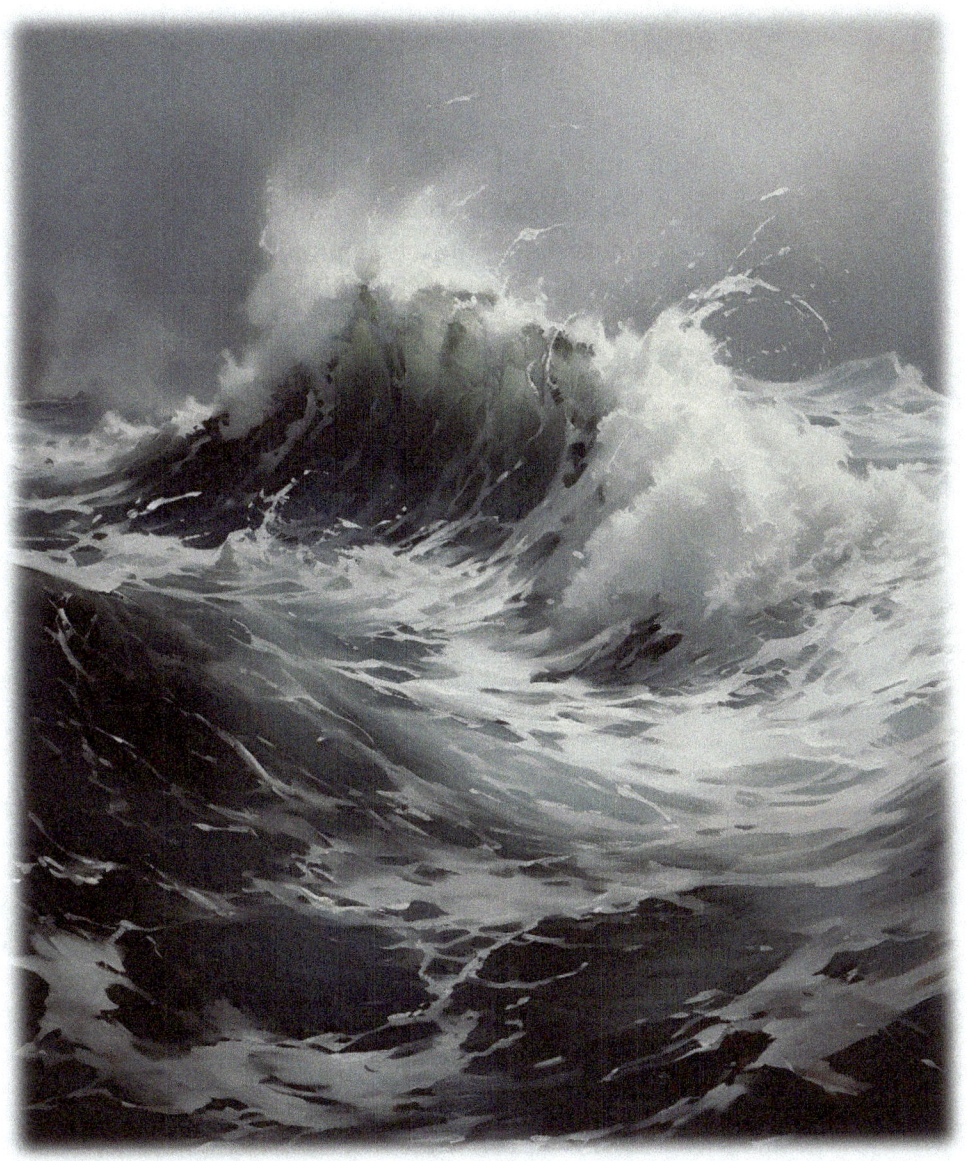

"Forgotten"

In dusk's veil, whispers hail,
A tale of silence, rides in rail.
Mourners gather, unseen, untold,
It is a funeral, secrets hold.

Beneath the moon's mournful glow,
A grave unmarked, life's echo.
Candles flicker, a ghostly show,
For a soul forgotten, below.

Echoes fade, a forgotten light,
In the hush tones, eternal night.
A spirit's journey, out of sight,
In death's embrace, takes flight.

Stars weep, velvet sky,
As time whispers a final goodbye.
In the realm of the lost, secrets lie,
At the funeral of the forgotten
A last goodbye.

IMMER CALLISTO

THE HANG-ONE

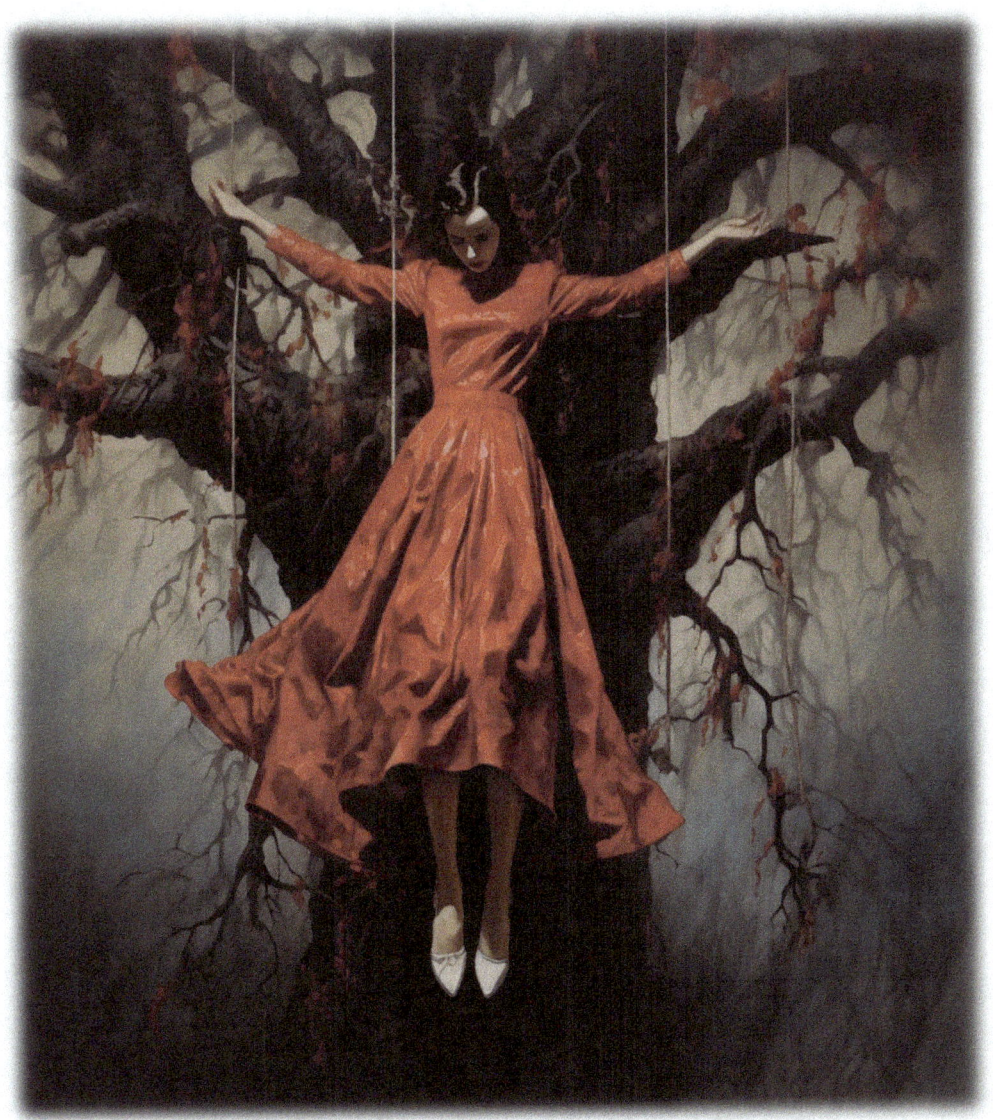

"Society's demand"

This world where norms demand a dance,
Each step measured, in life's strict glance.
To stray from the path, a daring stance,
Labeled insane, in society's expanse.

Different minds, colors bright and bold,
In a grey world, stories untold.
Yet to be oneself, daring and cold,
Is to walk in fire, break the mold.

It's a freedom, raw and rare,
To live true, in open air.
But in this truth, burdens bear,
For society's gaze is hard to bear.

Outside the lines, a lonely trail,
Where judgment storms, and criticisms hail.
Yet in this chaos, spirits prevail,
In the hell of norms, the different sail.

IMMER CALLISTO

THE PUPPETS

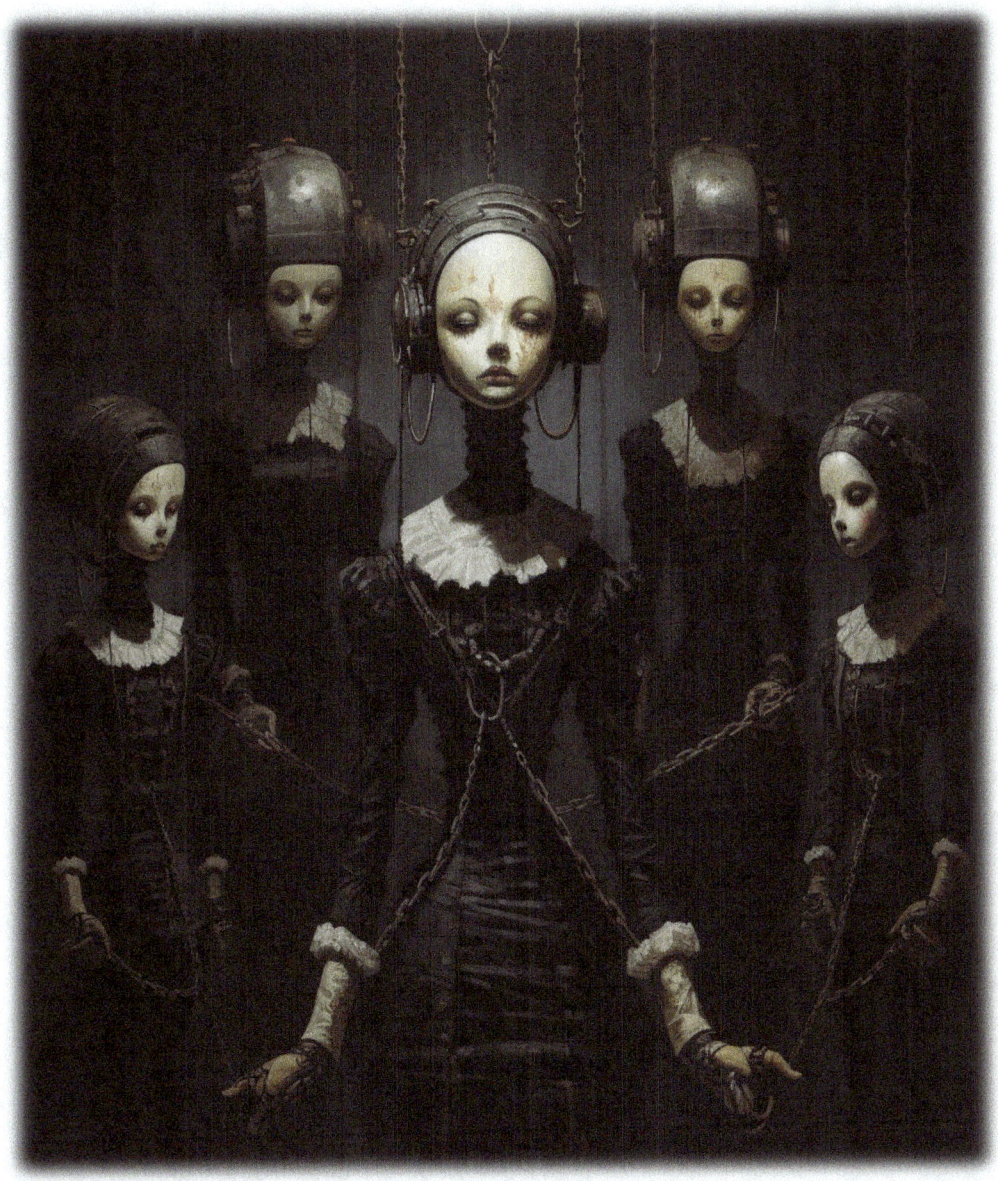

"A Heart's Quest"

In solitude, a heart does ache,
Years heavy, with sorrow in its wake.
A missing half, she yearns to make,
But love eludes, in the void's opaque.

Through endless nights, her steps do trace,
A quest for love, through time and space.
Destiny's chains, with cruel embrace,
Leave dreams of love, a fading grace.

Her tears, like rain, in silent plea,
Beguile the stars, her lone decree.
A soul's lament, in endless sea,
Longing for what cannot be.

THE LOVERS

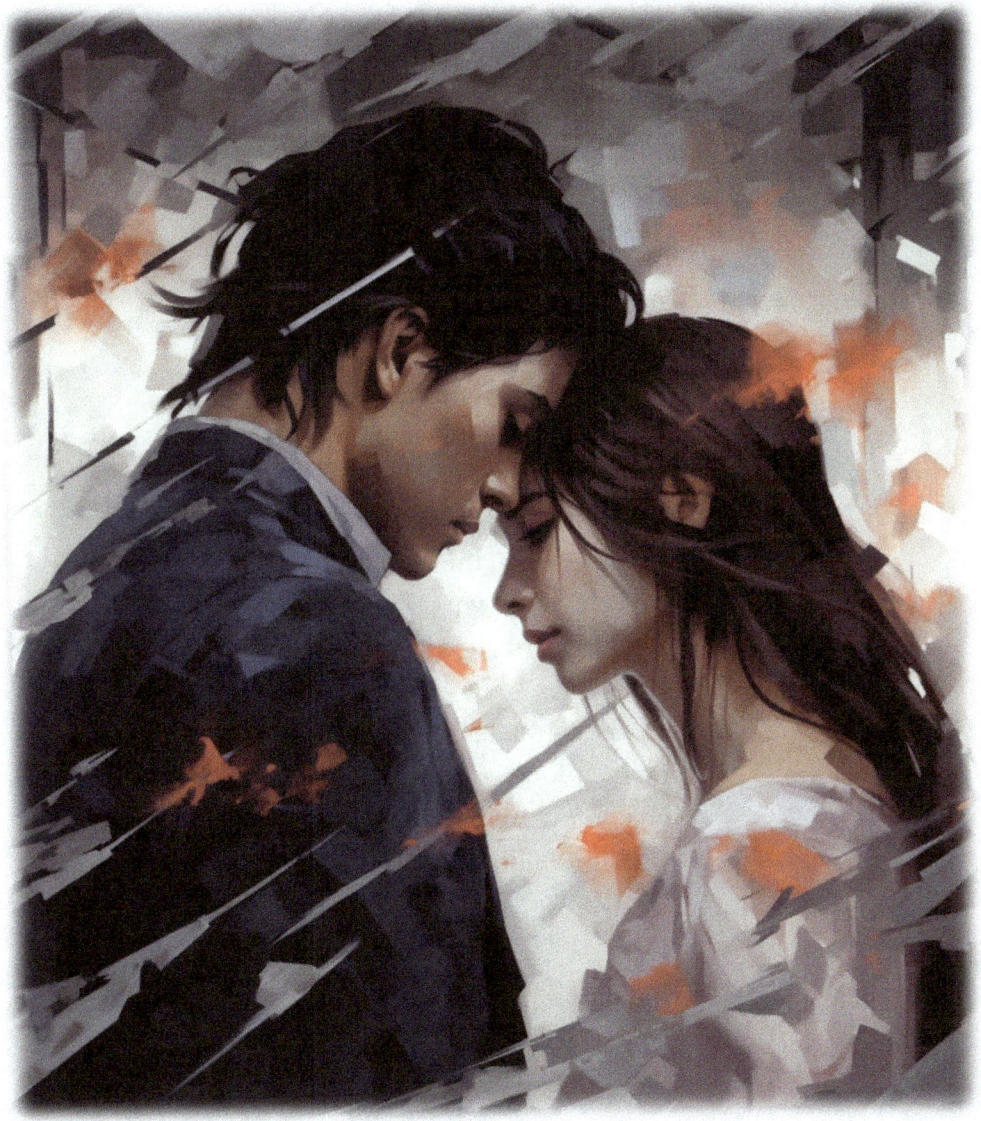

"Within"

Since childhood, dreams of true love spun,
To walk this earth, two hearts as one.
Believed in soulmates, twin flames' lure,
Heaven's test, love's essence pure.

Time passed, obstacles, rocks in my way,
Stumbled, hurled, a painful display.
First rock, not the one, yet three angels graced,
The sky gifted me, in love embraced.

Second rock, a mountain's cruel height,
Drowned me in pain, the crushing plight.
Had to release, for my soul's sake,
Tears flowed, heartache's relentless ache.

Dreams of soulmates, began to fade,
Standing alone, a stark cascade.
Then a revelation, a truth unbent,
Soulmate found, in self-content.

Alone, yet not, my soul's true mate,
Self-love discovered, an eternal state.

IMMER CALLISTO

THE MOON

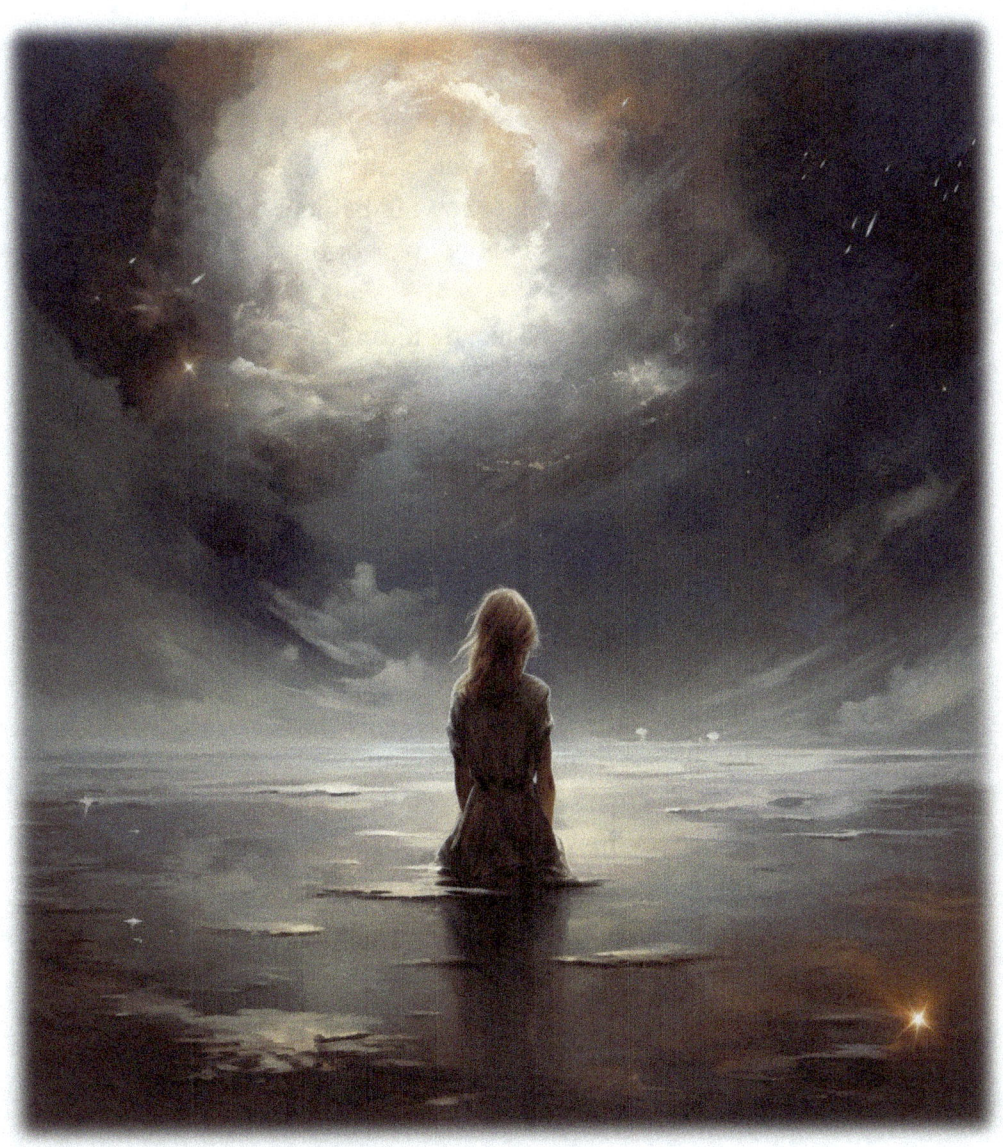

"In Her Shadow"

In shadows cast by mother's light,
I sought a father's love, an elusive flight.
His steps echoed, following behind,
Lost in her radiance, his love confined.

Yearning for his gaze, a guiding hand,
In her orbit, his presence stands.
I'd search within his silent gaze,
But Mother led, his existence in her terrain.

A longing for a bond, his heart's embrace,
Yet tethered to her, his quiet place.
In every glance, his eyes spoke her name,
His love, in her sphere, forever aflame.

In the dance of their intertwined fate,
Father's love seemed an endless wait.
Seeking solace in his arms,
I found nothing but her shadows bait.

Father's love, hah, what an elusive wait.

IMMER CALLISTO

THE INNOCENT

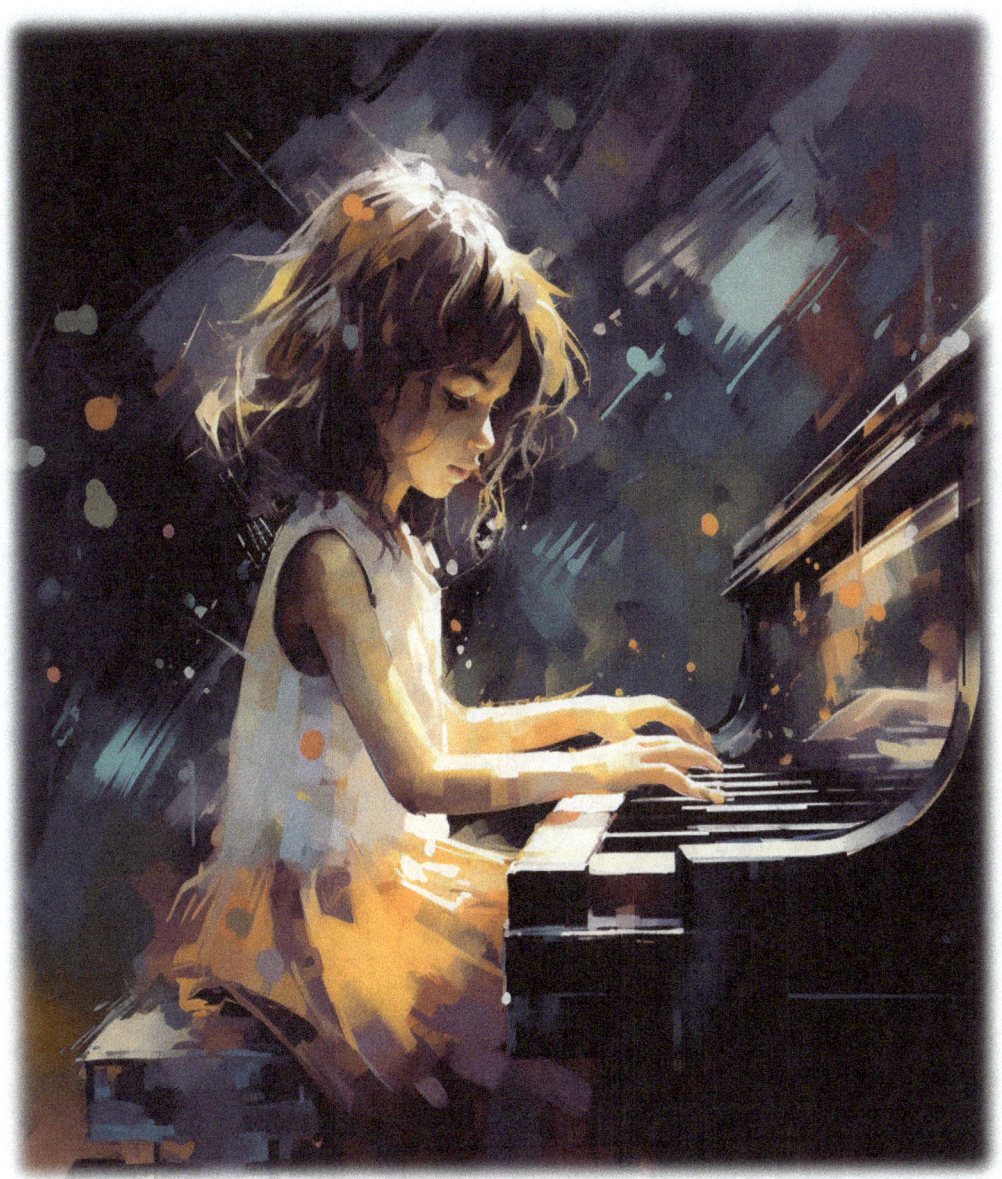

"The Narcissist"

Within his charm, a mesmerizing gaze I found,
A world of allure where my heart was bound.
Drawn by his charisma, a captivating art,
But his love was a deceitful, painful start.

A narcissist's guise, alluring and bright,
Masked the darkness, the shadows in the light.
In his reflection, I lost myself each day,
A toxic allure, leading my heart astray.

Every word spun, a web of crafted lies,
Ensnared in his charm, beneath sunny skies.
His love, a mirage, an illusionary play,
Leaving scars, in his manipulative display.

Recovery, a journey through tear-stained nights,
Breaking free from his manipulative sights.
Painful healing, reclaiming shattered parts,
Relearning love's truth, freeing chained hearts.

IMMER CALLISTO

THE NARCISSIST

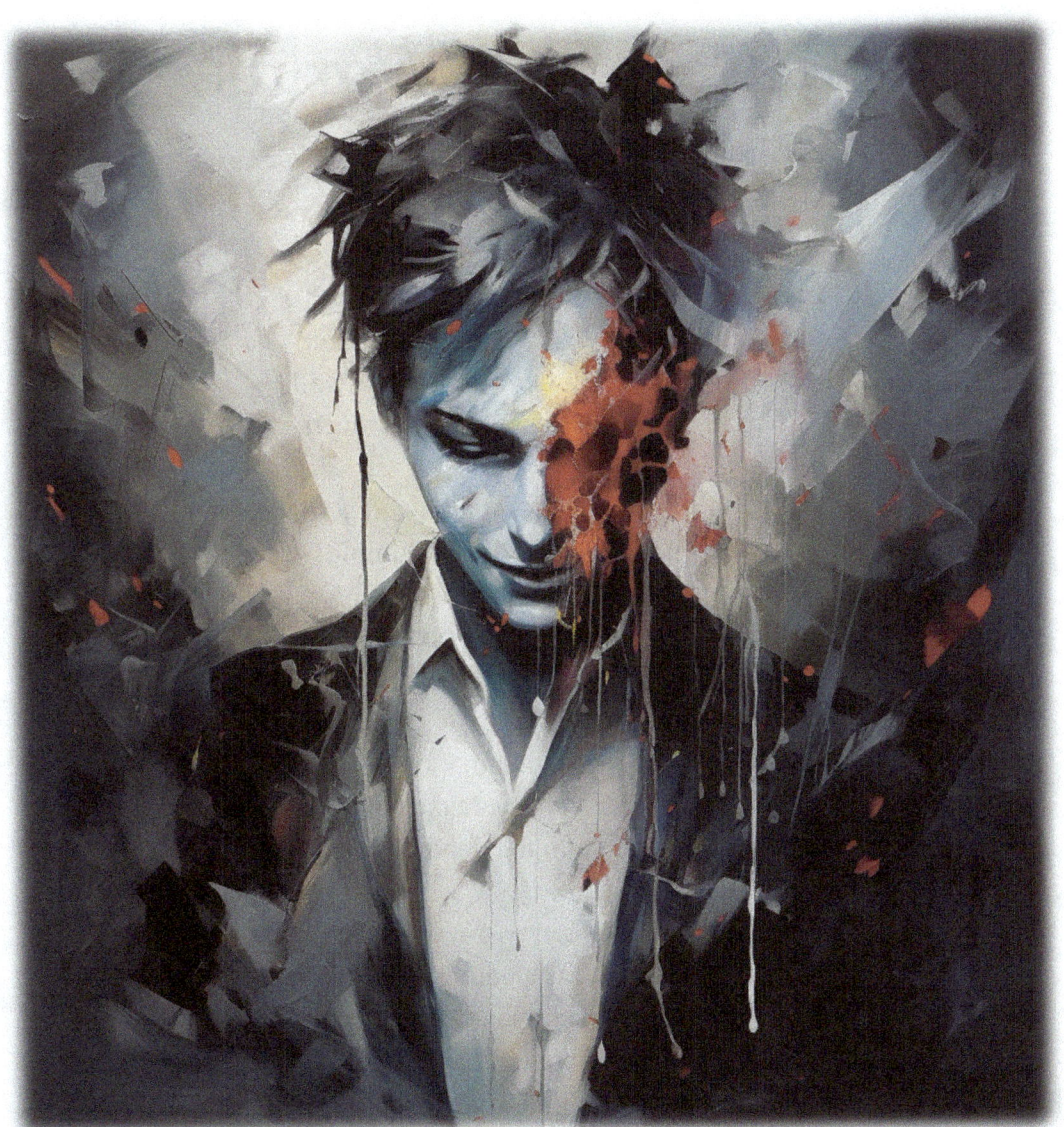

"Between Two Worlds"

In a realm where reality and dreams collide,
Lives a young girl with a world inside.
A universe vast in her mind does dwell,
But in her home, disbelief does swell.

Her family, the critics, harsh and cold,
Mock her tales, her dreams untold.
In their eyes, just childish play,
They cannot see her world's array.

Alone she stands, her pen her sword,
In the silence, her imagination soared.
In secret, her fantasies take flight,
Creating realms in the dead of night.

A young girl, between two worlds she lies,
In one scorned, in the other, she flies.
Her journey, a testament to her alone,
In her tales, her worth is shown.

IMMER CALLISTO

THE WRITER

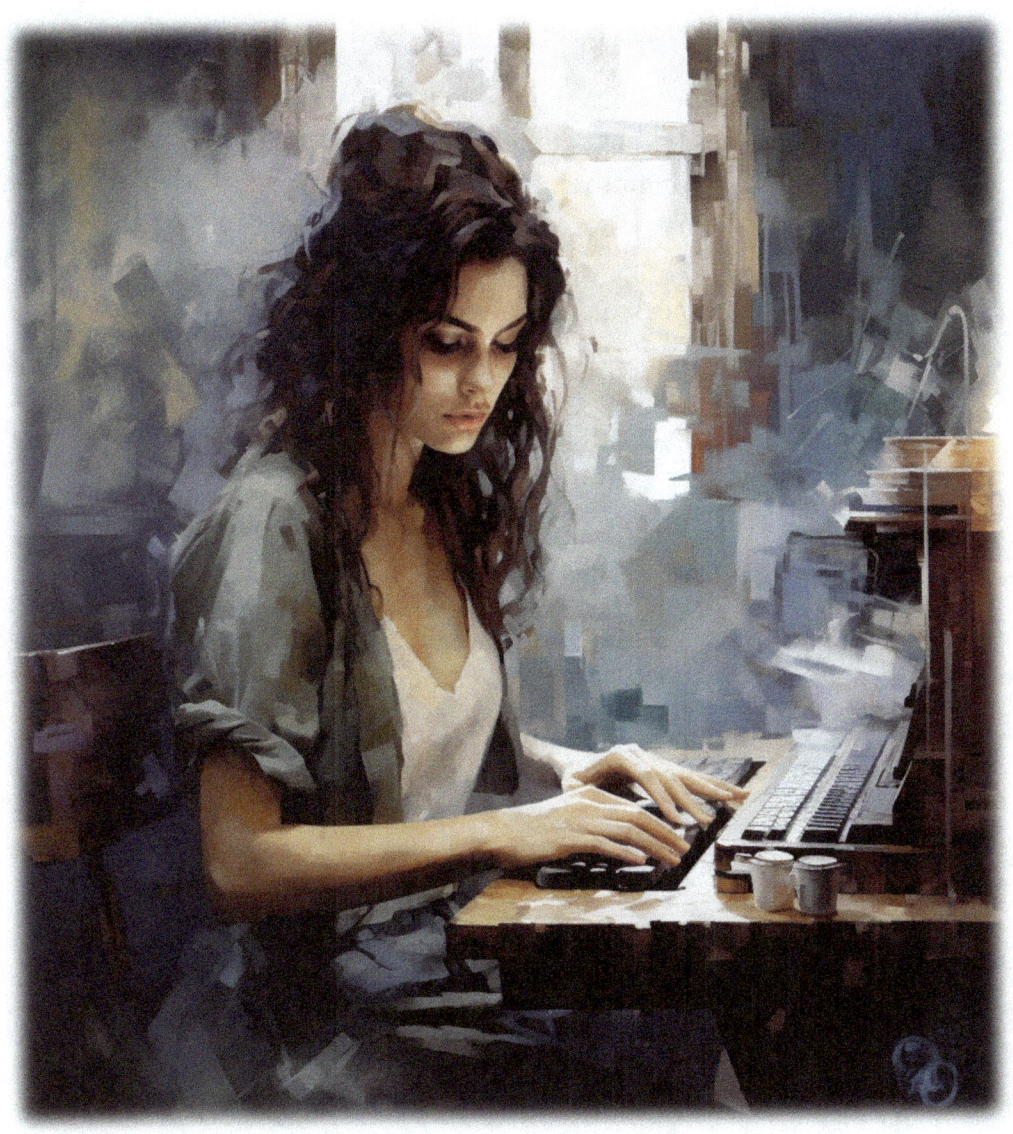

"Divergent Paths"

In a family where faith's light shines bright,
I walk a different path, in the moon's soft light.
Where hymns rise high, in solemn song,
I find my peace, where shadows belong.

They speak of one way, a narrow view,
But in my heart, a different truth grew.
In the quiet of nature, under starlit skies,
I found my calling, where my spirit lies.

Meditation's peace, a solace deep,
A practice they condemn, a leap.
Crystals' energy, in colors bold,
A magic they don't understand untold.

In their world, my ways seem dark,
A path of shadows, an offbeat mark.
Yet in this divergence, my identity sparks,
In pagan rites, my true journey starts.

In their eyes, I may be the crazy one,
A soul untamed, a different sun.
But in my heart, I know my truth,
I'm a pagan spirit, in eternal youth.

THE PHOENIX

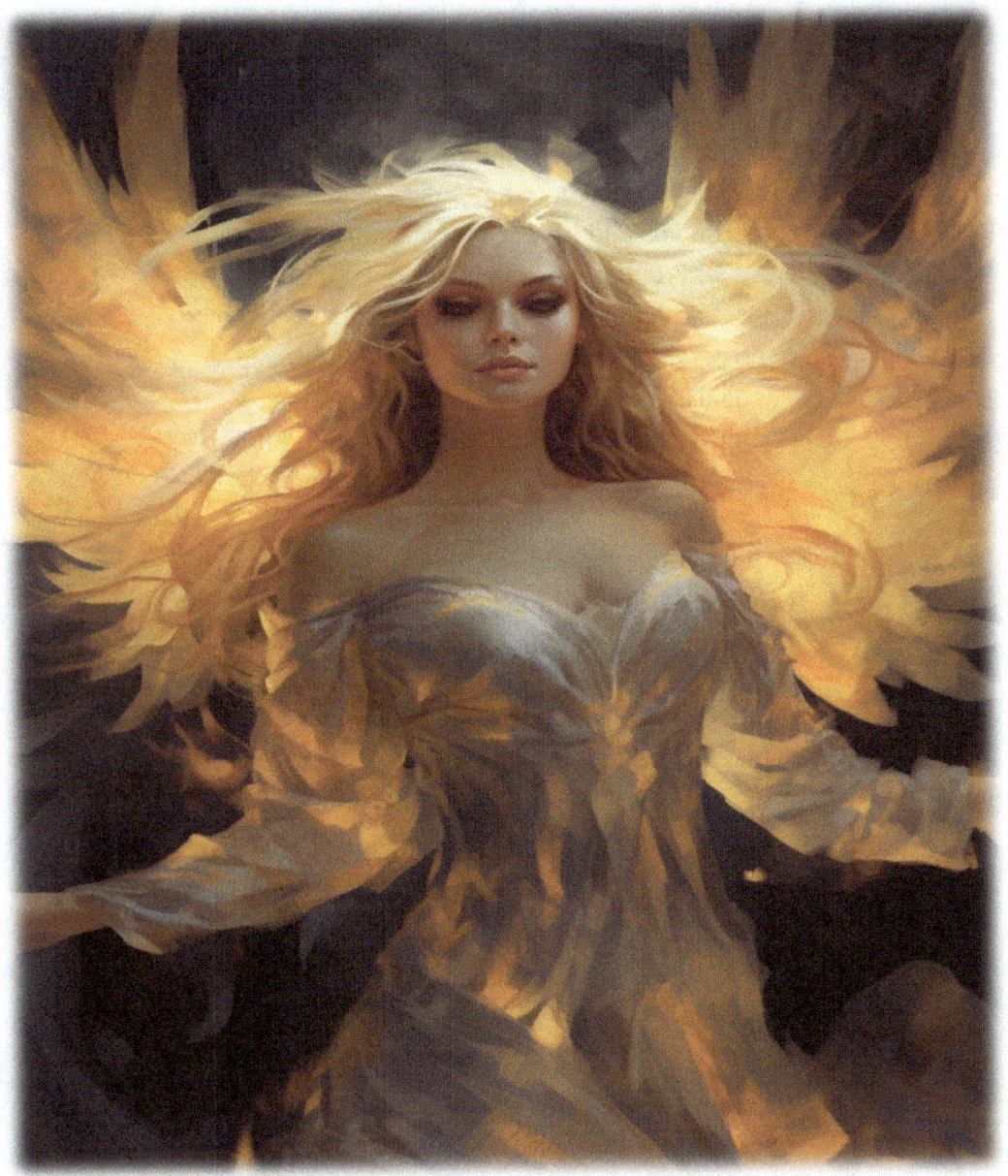

"Running Away"

During the stillness of night, she slipped away,
From the home where loneliness held sway.
Friends and kin, yet a heart adrift,
Aching voids, a silent rift.

To the park she fled, seeking solace's embrace,
A chance encounter, a girl's searching face.
Eyes met, a mother's warmth she longed to know,
Yearning for love's embrace to show.

The police found her, a tale unveiled,
A journey through darkness, truths prevailed.
A kind couple's aid, a guiding light,
Leading her back, from the lonely night.

Home, she returned, to the familiar place,
Yet in her heart, the void held its space.
The warmth of family, an elusive grace,
Loneliness lingered, in life's embrace.

IMMER CALLISTO

THE RUNAWAY

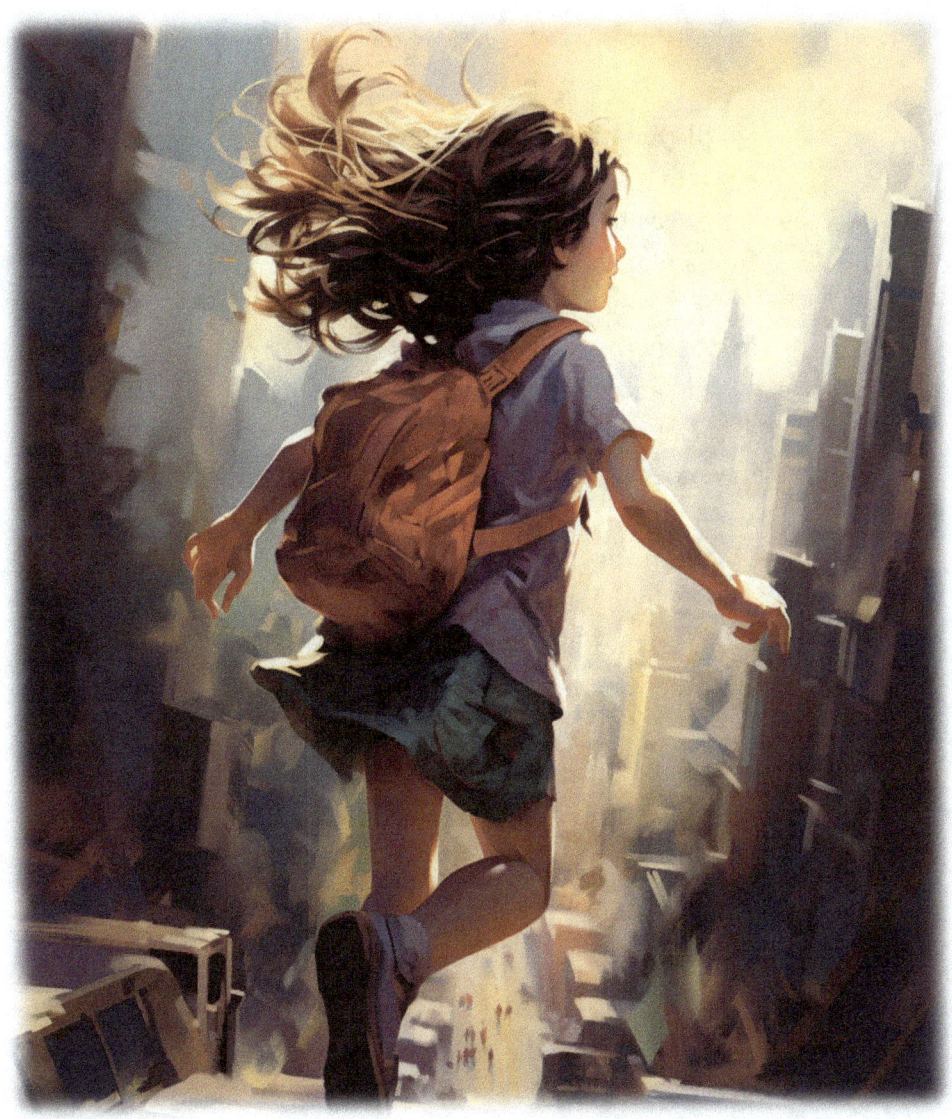

"Facade of Love"

He played his part, In the game of hearts,
With a sly grin and a cheating heart.
I was his second, a hidden flame,
In his world of deceit, a shadowed game.

He whispered sweet nothings, a crafted art,
While another held the lead in his heart.
But even as I rose to be his first,
His wandering eye continued its cursed thirst.

With me as his queen, or so it seemed,
His love was but a fleeting dream.
For in the shadows, he sought anew,
Another heart to ensnare, a love untrue.

I realized then, his love was a maze,
A labyrinth of lies, a heartless craze.
As he found another, to take my place,
I saw the truth, behind his face.

IMMER CALLISTO

THE CHEATER

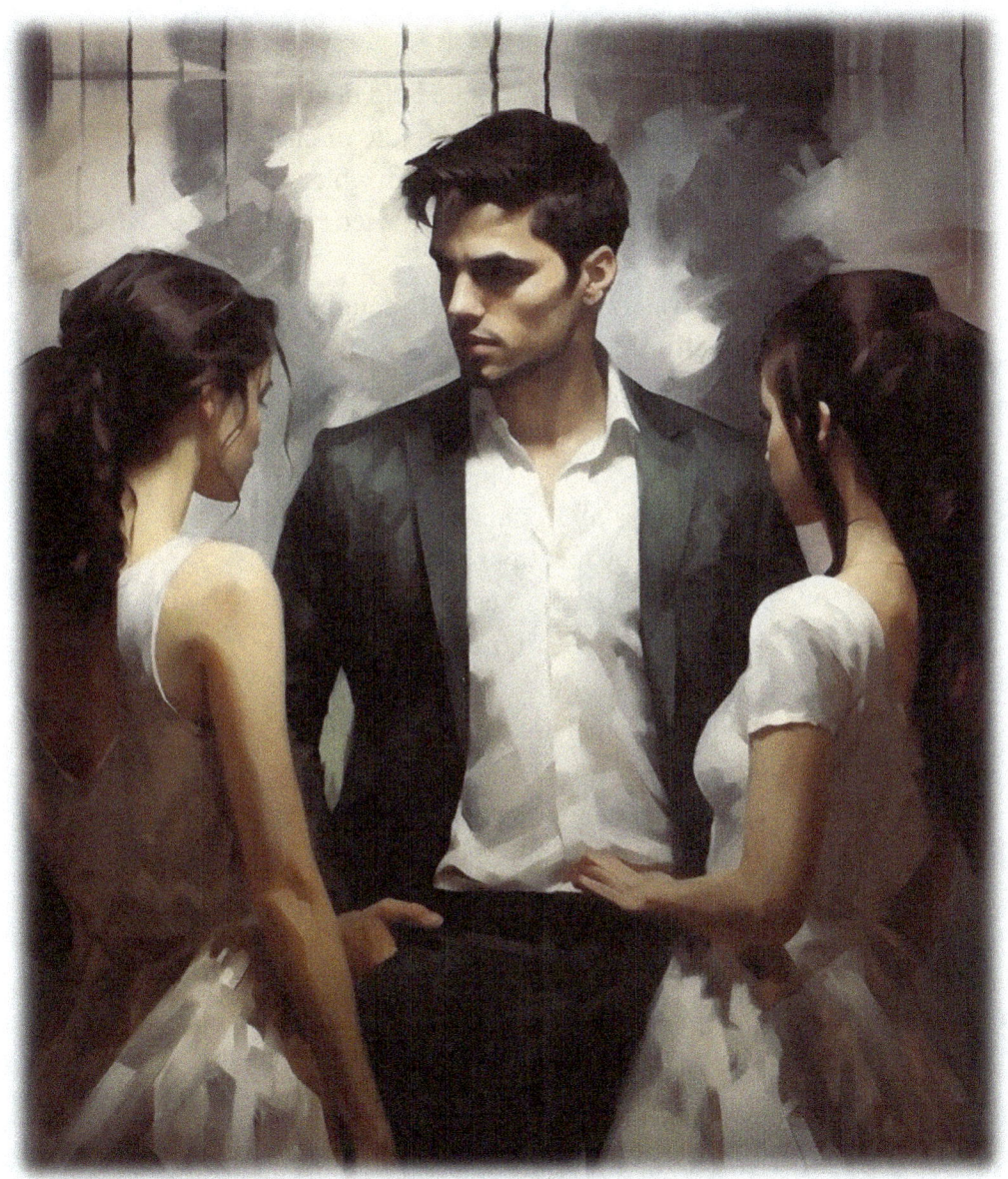

"A Puppy's Love"

Searching for love once held dear,
I brought home a puppy, a bundle of cheer.
A tiny soul with eyes so bright,
In his little paws, my world turned right.

He wasn't for me, or so I thought,
A gift of love, in kindness bought.
Yet in his wagging tail, a story spun,
Of a bond unexpected, second to none.

Through days of gloom and lonely nights,
He stood by me, my beacon of light.
With every bark, every playful leap,
He soothed my heart, no longer to weep.

His joyful yaps, his comforting nuzzle,
In times of despair, he was my puzzle's muzzle.
In his innocent eyes, a world of glee,
A faithful companion, he came to be.

IMMER CALLISTO

THE COMPANION

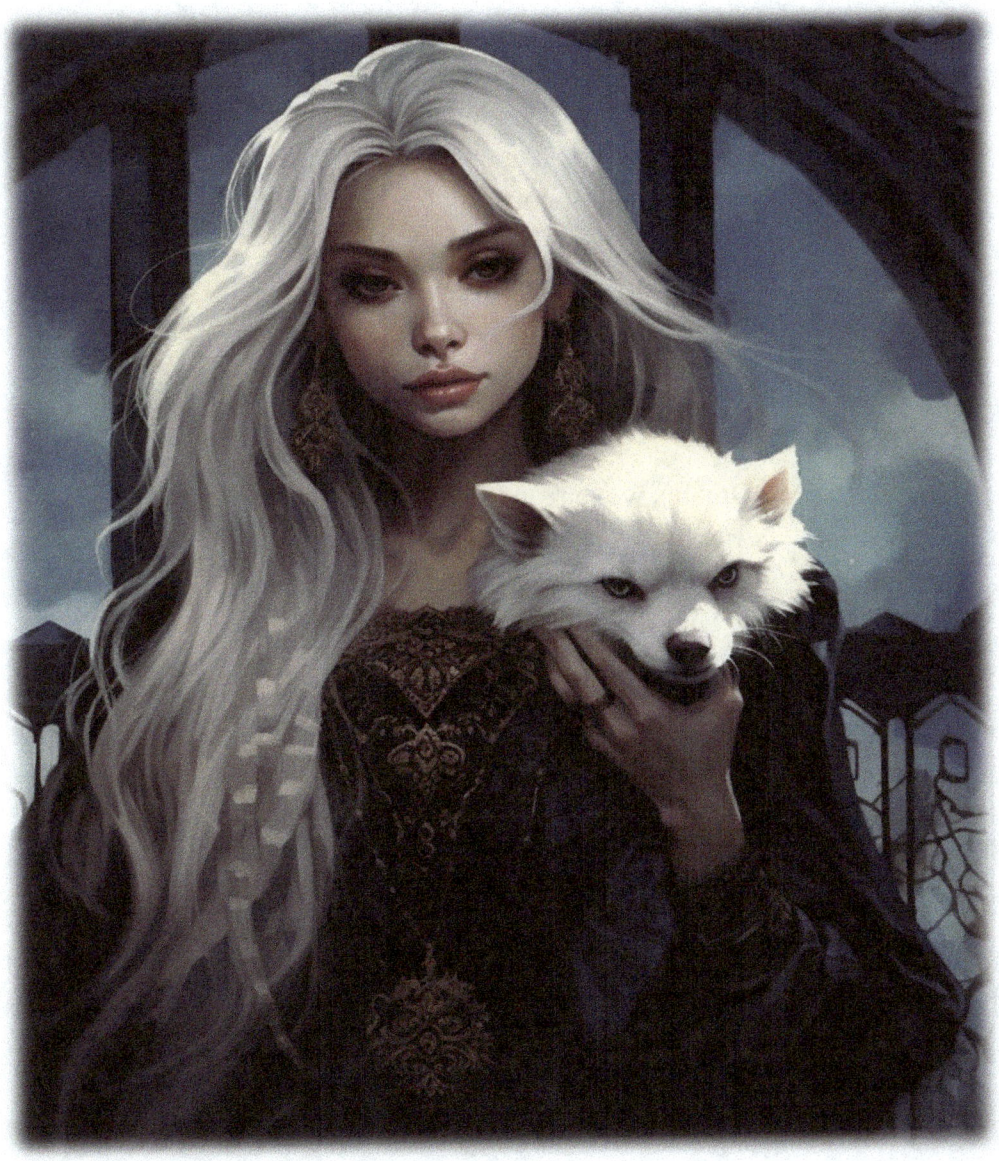

"A Love Await"

In the shadows of heartbreak's stain,
I find myself in a loveless terrain.
Darkness looms in every man I meet,
None resonates, none my heart can greet.

Not my ex, nor any in my sight,
My heart veers away, longing for light.
For there's another, not from this sphere,
A being from realms I hold dear.

Dreams woven since I was but a child,
An otherworldly love, gentle and mild.
He came for me, from a distant place,
Unaware, yet my heart does race.

Growing old in the endless wait,
Yearning for a love, destined fate.
He's my one, my only true love's glow,
In this world together, yet he doesn't know.

IMMER CALLISTO

THE WORLD

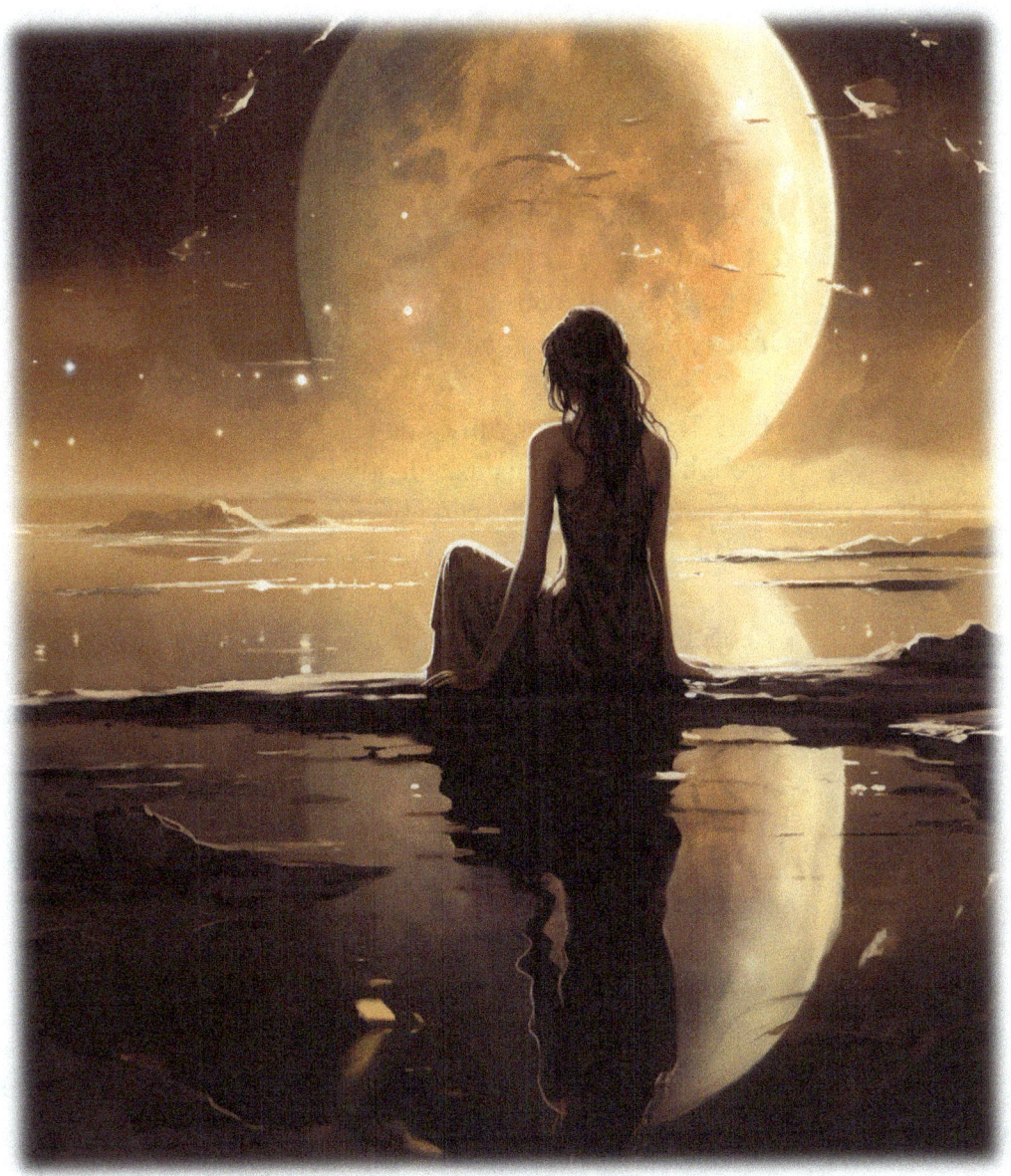

"In the Shadows of the Night"

DARK shadows, under the moon's light,
Came a black kitten, a magical sight.
With eyes like embers, glowing bright,
In his graceful steps, the world felt right.

NIGHT after night, by my side he stayed,
Through spells and chants, silently he laid.
A familiar bond, in secret we made,
In his, a kindred spirit, never to fade.

Together we explored realms unseen,
In moonlit rituals, where I've always been.
His eyes, a guide in the dark, a sheen,
With him, I embraced what I truly mean.

In the dance of shadows, with him by my side,
In ancient rites, in nature's stride,
I found my truth, no longer to hide,
With my black kitten, forever my guide.

IMMER CALLISTO

THE BLACK CAT

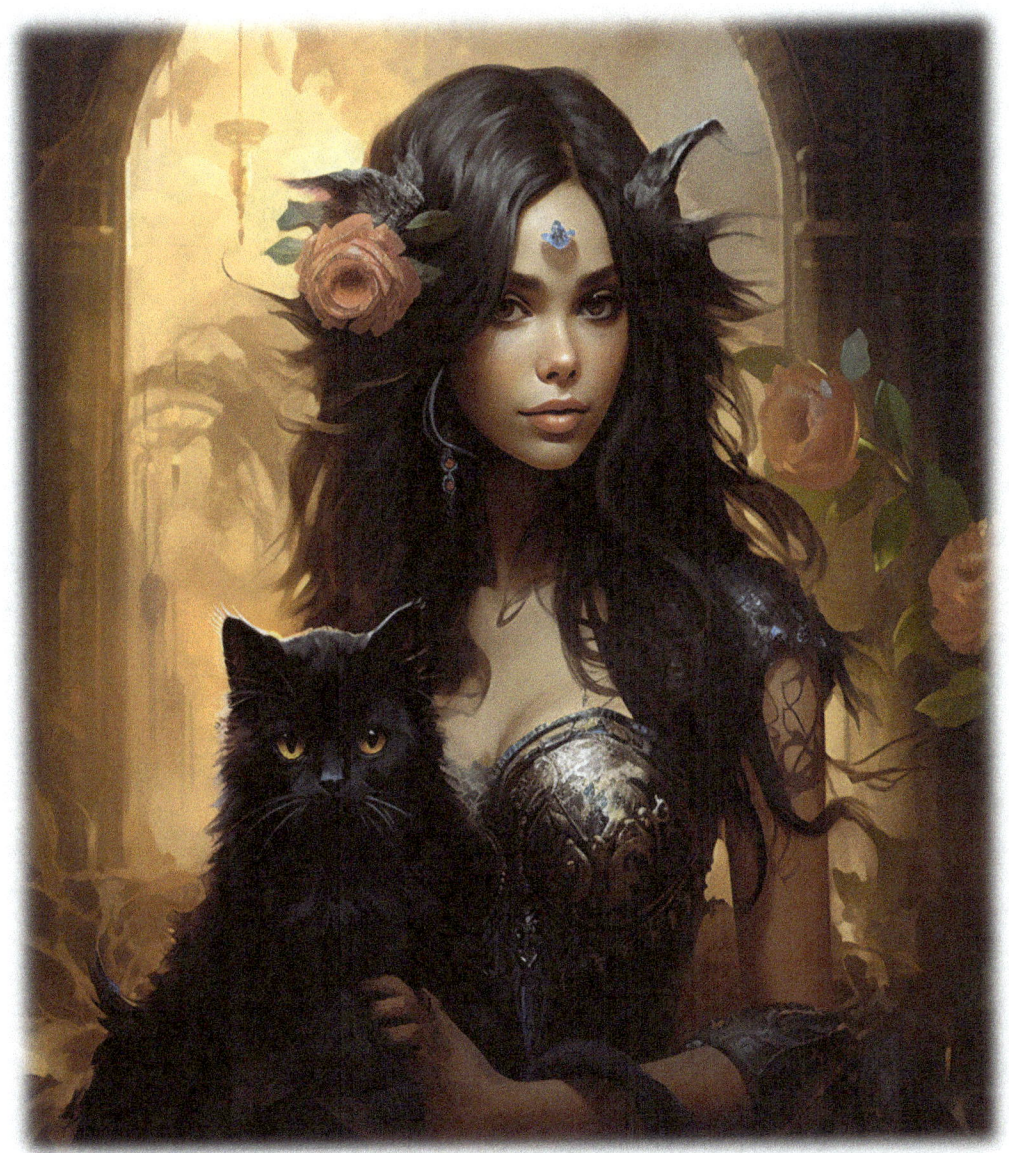

"Guardians of Tomorrow's Minds"

In halls of learning, they stand firm, unsung,
Crafting futures with heart and tongue.
Teachers, guardians of the mind's young bloom,
In their care, the seeds of tomorrow loom.

Sculpting dreams from the clay of youth,
They wield knowledge to uncover truth.
Yet often their worth goes unseen,
In the quiet toil of the classroom scene.

Now I join this noble fray,
Feeling the weight of each teaching day.
But in this labor, my passion's found,
With every lesson, my purpose is sound.

May I grow old with chalk in hand,
Guiding seekers to understand.
For in each child's eager eyes,
Lies the teacher's cherished prize.

IMMER CALLISTO

THE FOOL

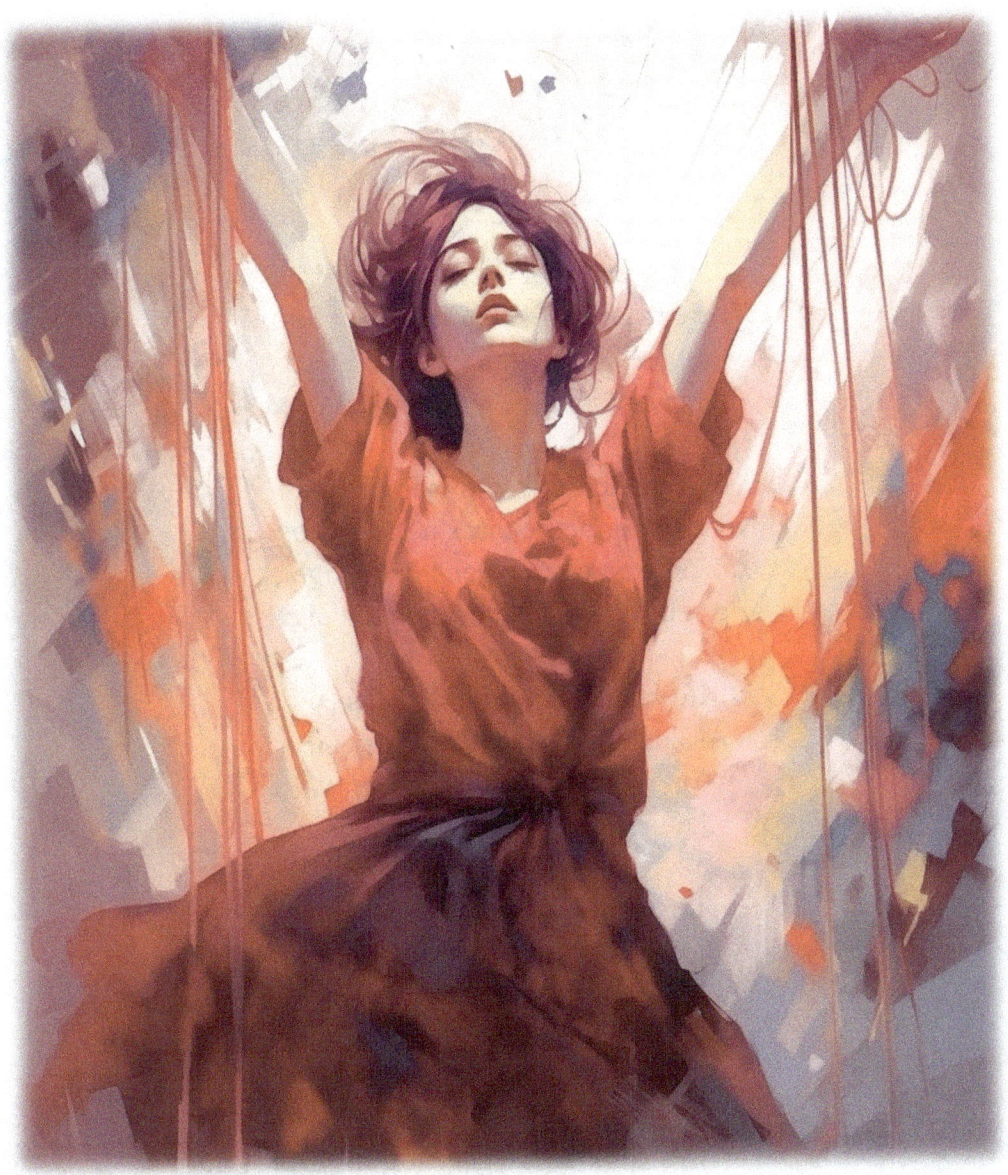

"Whispers of a Kinder Sphere"

In the realm of my silent yearn,
Where the tides of avarice do not turn,
A sphere beyond the green of greed,
Where want is filled with selfless deed.

No thunder of war to mar the sky,
No tears for peace that's passed us by,
A land where hues blend in the light,
And souls are judged not by their sight.

Strife, though present, finds its end,
As hand to hand, we all befriend.
Toil weaves the bonds of unity,
In the fabric of a shared community.

In this world, my heart does roam,
A dreamer's wish for a kinder home,
Where wealth is counted by love's measure,
And every breath is life's true treasure.

IMMER CALLISTO

THE TRAVELER

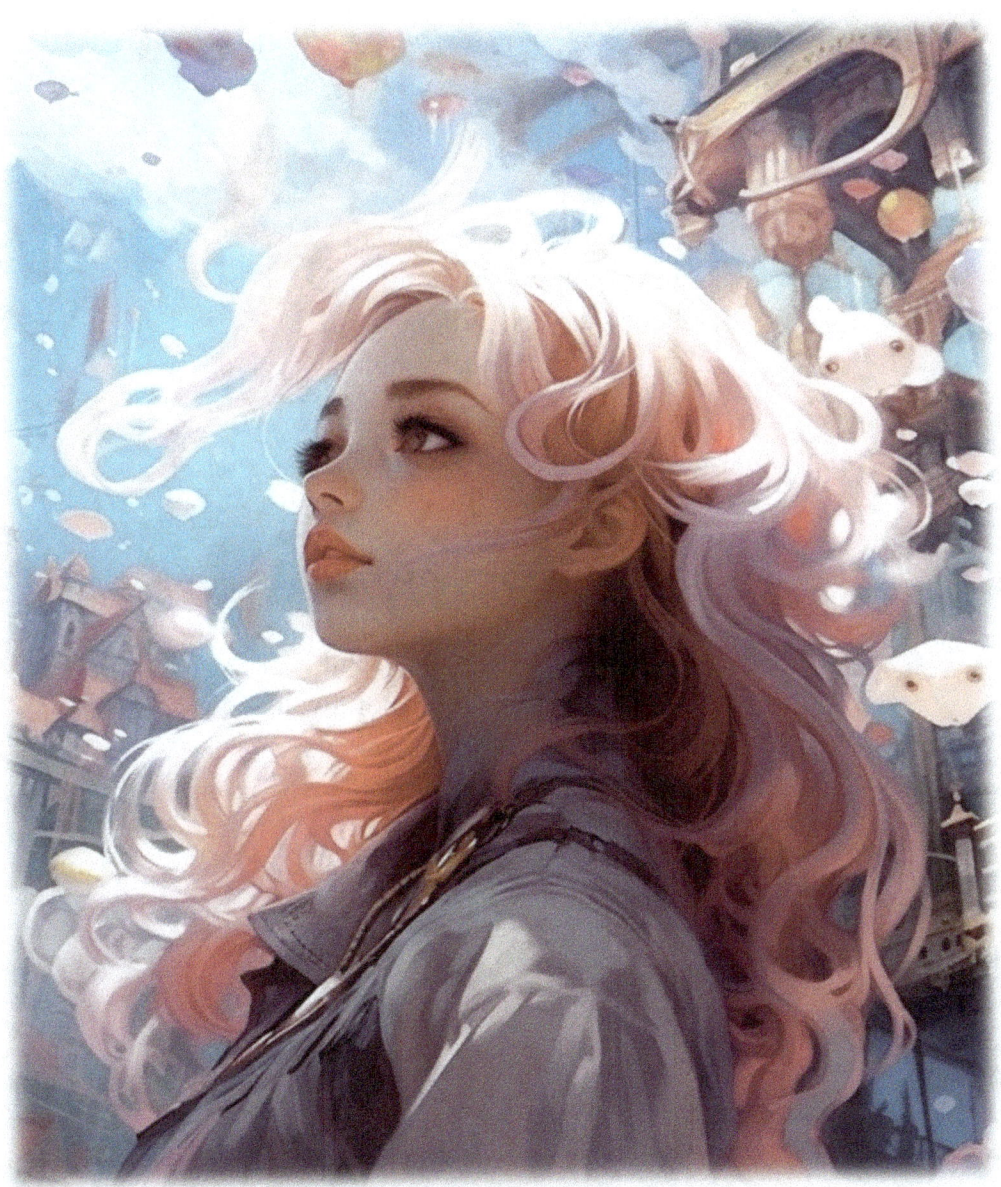

"Time Fails"

In the realm where seconds fall away,
A land untouched by night or day,
Time's a river, ever flowing,
Yet its passage, never showing.

Here, in this eternal dance,
Moments neither pause nor advance.
An illusion, finely spun,
Underneath an ageless sun.

In this world, a timeless spell,
Where hours neither come nor dwell.
A whispered secret of the universe,
In the timeless poet's grail.

IMMER CALLISTO

THE TIMER

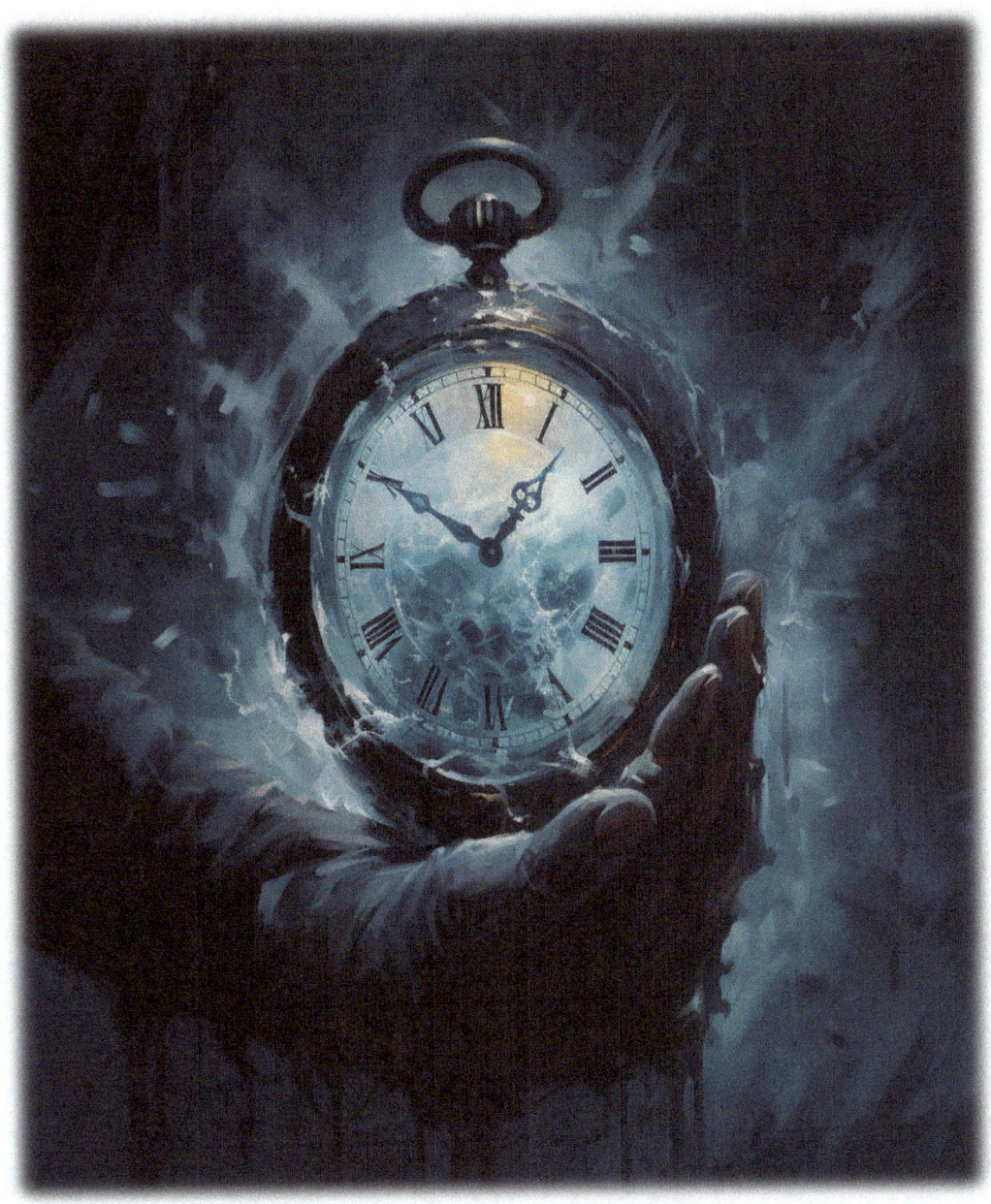

A Lesson in love

Watch for red flags in love's game,
They whisper of a future not the same.
True love's a path both must walk,
Not just one's dream, but a shared talk.

Love is lovely when it's two,
A shared journey, feelings true.
But first, love yourself, stand alone,
Only then is love's true beauty shown.

Forget the chase for gold and fame,

For wealth in life is not the same.
Treasures true aren't counted in gold,
But in the joys we hold and mold.

Be thankful for the air, the sky,
For every laugh, each tear we cry.
Riches found in love's embrace,
In simple moments, life's true grace.

A millionaire in heart and soul,
With gratitude playing the vital role.
In every sunrise, every star's gleam,
Find the wealth in life's simple dream.

In the labyrinth of the mind,

Seeking help is not confined.
Mental health, a precious key,
Unlocking doors to set us free.

Depression's shadow, real and deep,
A challenge steep, but not too steep.
Reach out, speak, let it be known,
No one should face this path alone.

Let's embrace this vital truth,
In every elder, in every youth:
Healing starts with a spoken plea,
In asking help, we find the key.

FAREWELL

In this parting, let words be sweet,

A journey ends, yet again we'll meet.

In every goodbye, a promise anew,

Till next time, in the heart's fond view.

Thank you!

To those who've wandered through my art and verse,
Whose hearts have danced to the rhythm of my universe,
I send my thanks on wings of time,
In grateful cadence, with a hint of thyme.

Your eyes and souls, in kindred flare,
Have seen beyond what's simply there.
So, with a bow and a poet's chime,
I thank you deeply, in seasoned rhyme.

The end...
To a
New beginning

www.ingramcontent.com/pod-product-compliance
Lightning Source LLC
Chambersburg PA
CBHW060533010626
45794CB00022B/2408